HELP!
Motivation for the Mind, Body and Soul

HELP!

Motivation for the Mind, Body and Soul

Gregory V. Arnold

An Avenue of Creative Thoughts to Help
Lost Individuals Navigate Through a Life of
Road Blocks and Dead Ends

Copyright 2009 by Gregory V. Arnold

All rights reserved. Published 2009.

Printed in the United States of America

Help Enterprises
P.O. Box 431562
Los Angeles, CA 90043
323-833-1588
www.helpmehelpyouhelpus.com

LCCN: 2009937317

ISBN: 978-0-615-32385-5

CONTENTS

Introduction — vii

Chapter One — 1
Love Thyself

Chapter Two — 23
Where Do We Go From Here?

Chapter Three — 49
God Help Us!

Chapter Four — 69
Faith, Dreams and Aspirations

Chapter Five — 93
The Blues! (Constructive Criticism)

Chapter Six — 115
Wherewithal (By Any Means Necessary)

Chapter Seven — 133
Self-Defense!

Chapter Eight — 163
Bad Habits Die Slowly

Chapter Nine — 187
Hell on Earth (September 11, 2001)

Chapter Ten — 199
Divine Guidance!

Chapter Eleven — 221
Bliss!

help (help), v.t. to give or provide what is necessary to accomplish a task or satisfy a need; contribute strength or means to; render assistance to; cooperate effectively with aid; assist.

INTRODUCTION

Help Me, Help You, Help Us!

My birth name, which was issued to me by teenage mother, is Gregory Vondell Arnold. The ideas, thoughts, and passion-filled words that are printed on these pages are my opinions and point of view based on my personal experiences and research. My goal is to explore honesty and remove mental shackles from a self-imposed prison reality. I will highlight an array of topics that I believe has created "Hell on Earth" for the majority of the human race. I have labeled my constructive criticism to the world as "The Blues." I choose to use my words as instruments, and I trust my perspective will orchestrate music to your ears. I am not out to blame any one race, but I will highlight well-documented history that is known throughout the world. I offer this motivational book to be used as a tool to help motivate your mind, body, and soul. As you journey through the pages, travel with an open mind and honestly ask yourself these questions: Do these circumstances apply to me? Am I a part of the problem or am I part of the solution? And the last and most important question: What can I do to expedite a positive outcome?

It will take our whole community to tackle the issues we face as humans. I am only one concerned citizen, and I have chosen to take a stand and speak what I believe in my heart is right. My belief is faith based, and I am willing to be accountable for my actions. If you wish to make a change in your

HELP!

life, it is all up to you. I was once "The World Champion of Procrastination," now I get out in the world and get things done. My energy is out of this world because I now believe in me. Today I stand independent through mind, body, and soul — all being blessed by God. All religions are more than welcome to read this motivational book. THIS IS NOT A RELIGIOUS DOCTRINE! This is a faith-based memoir that has been created to aid those in need of a helping hand. As you read this book, feel free to replace the word God with whomever YOU worship. My God is my God, and YOU have the choice to call God whatever you see fit to save your soul. This book is intended for universal use for our entire society.

On the Format of This Book

Our "thoughts" are derived from our conscious based in the emotions of an individual idea. Our "afterthoughts" are derived from our subconscious based in experienece and what we believe at the moment to be factual.

The first section of each individual page in this book represents the thought, and the second section represents the afterthought. HELP! is an account of my personal thoughts and aftertoughts based on thirty-five years of life experience.

CHAPTER ONE

Love Thyself

Chapter 1 gives you the courage to challenge the expectations of society and educate your self-esteem to tutor your conscious and subconscious. It is crucial to comprehend this first entry because it allows you to accept the perception of people's assumptions. You will realize through your own observation that it does not matter what people think about you, it only matters how you feel about those unnecessary thoughts. The overall objective is to create a balanced person who has passion, purpose, and a philosophy of self-value through humbleness. The more humble you become; the more it will become a habit to accept and acknowledge how beautiful you are. This opportunity is a chance of a lifetime, which allows you to fall in love with YOU.

HELP!

The Damage Is Done, So Resurrect Your Beautiful Being

Today we will collect the fragments of our life and mold happiness. Organize your life, and God will bless the birth of a new beginning with bliss. You have to envision yourself three steps ahead while you crawl to your feet. Begin your journey with a pace that commands comfort and accelerates as you go. Make an assertive effort to smile in the mirror, which will embrace a delicate ego. Concentrate on the characteristics that make you feel good about being you. Repel the thoughts that spread cancer through the mind, body, and soul. Look upon your life and limit the negative energy that you put out into the world. Infuse your conscious with positive passion, and the joy will lead to self-esteem. Believe in yourself and your ability to achieve the spirituality God issued to each of us equally. Pave a path of love to your heart that exits the highway to healing. Love begins in the soul of the individual who exercises faith. Love is everlasting when it begins and ends with God. The objective to life is to love thyself, since you share your lifetime with no other entity but God.

CHAPTER 1: LOVE THYSELF

Is It Time to Reevaluate Your World?

The vision that you view in the mirror is the sight of the individual you have manifested. If you do not embrace, love, and respect the reflection that you see, then now is the time to reevaluate your world. Invest time in exploring the structure of your life. Look into your family history and the achievements of your ancestors. Take pride in who, what, and where you come from. When you choose to embrace strengths and weaknesses, the picture in the mirror will become crystal clear.

HELP!

Let God Be the Judge

Tell yourself: "I will no longer allow another to dictate my opinion of myself. My only concern as I move forward is how I demonstrate my daily deeds to God." There is no one who can judge you but God. Do not waste time creating self-doubt in your own mind.

CHAPTER 1: LOVE THYSELF

Anything Is within Your Reach

Pressure is the cancer of ability and acquisition. Imagination will allow the virus to spread agony if you don't believe in yourself. Any task or objective can be obtained when you focus on the goal at hand. Invest quality effort in your target and allow your mind to penetrate the bull's-eye. You can accomplish anything you wish, once you utilize your heart and soul.

HELP!

When I Finally Found Myself, I Realized That I Was Best by Myself

A famous rhythm and blues singer said it best: "I think I better let it go." Lost love can not be captured by a compass or nestled by a net. The love that is truly yours will wrestle away all troubles and concerns. Love is eternal and does not evaporate from heat and tension. There is no greater love than a personal emotion for yourself. Salvage yourself from all your past failures, faults, and emotional scars; do not waste away in a love/hate relationship with yourself. Spend time alone. Enjoy the sweet sound of silence because family, friends, and foes synthesize music to the ears. You should love yourself regardless, even if for the moment you find yourself alone. Isolation affords the time to reflect on and repent for the shortcomings of our salvation. God will grant our grace as He grooms us for our genuine purpose in life.

CHAPTER 1: LOVE THYSELF

We Dictate the Wellness of Our Body; Fitness Is Vital to the Longevity of Life

Americans are addicted to drugs, alcohol, and bad eating habits. Both legal drugs approved by the government and illegal drugs condemned by society have a lasting effect on the user. Still, they both have a loyal following and generate billions of dollars in revenue for their manufacturers. Drugs of any kind have side effects. Prescription drugs are as addictive as powder cocaine, crack, and marijuana.

Alcohol abuse has murdered the inner city community at an alarming rate. While allowing the pressure of life to chase us to the bottle, our community has funded the cancer of our own people. The government seal is broken every time we purchase poison that has flooded into urban society.

Fast food, pork, and high-calorie snacks lead to an unhealthy diet. The human body can not operate properly when it is fueled from food that does not provide energy. We consume too much garbage that only builds fat and destroys muscle. We have to get off the couch and exercise to breathe fresh life into our bodies. A weak mind, body, and soul will allow life to evaporate right in front of our eyes.

HELP!

My Destiny Parallels My Desires by Multiplying My Tenacious Thoughts, by the Sum of My Command

A wish will wander until hope has its way. An aura of faith collides with cockiness claiming karma as collateral. Confidence is crucial in a society that aligns arrogance with courage. If it takes being vain to vanquish vulnerability, are you able to stand accused? An ordeal will often show the outside world the depth of your poise. You are capable of controlling your own cause and establishing an extraordinary effect by diminishing self-doubt.

CHAPTER 1: LOVE THYSELF

Do Not Allow Your Mind, Body and Soul to Be Digested in the Belly of the Beast

Society has conditioned individuals to live as followers. Our nation does not promote desire, dedication, or discipline. Life is bland without risk or the confidence to take a chance. Success is the ability to leave your comfort zone and allow action to dictate desire, dedication, or discipline. Education frees the mind and expands the desire for information. The body will begin to heal itself once hard work and dedication become a permanent fixture in your routine (eating responsibly and being active). God is the key to discipline; your faith will insist that you follow the laws of the land and live a righteous existence. You can only lead by example; you can not lead from behind.

HELP!

Do Not Glamorize the Actions of Others by Attempting to Imitate Them

The easiest task in the world is to be you. Do not fall victim to peer pressure from a follower. Life's experience can not be beneficial if you focus on shortcuts and always seek the easy way out. The old-fashioned method of hard work is less appealing to the masses, but true success is reached through the straight and narrow path. There is a limited space between joy and pain. I believe each individual has the power to issue value to what's important in his or her own life. You are an individual with God-given talent; so why not appreciate, admire, and love being who you are?

CHAPTER 1: LOVE THYSELF

To Thyself Be True; Why Do We Allow Love to Blind Us?

Why are we afraid of being alone? Why do we sacrifice our own happiness for a false sense of security? Why do we willingly do for someone that which we would not do for our own selves? Our conscious can command charity as an outlet to balance selfish behavior. The problem is sometimes we panic and purchase companionship at the cost of our courage. You can not afford to place your heart and soul into everybody. You can not genuinely love anyone if you do not love yourself first. Live in love—not in fear!

HELP!

You Will Tap into Your True Potential Once You Venture out on a Limb

Do not allow failure to stunt the growth of your self-esteem. You can not succeed or even fail, if you do not put forth any energy or effort. You have to enhance your inner being and destroy your self-imposed limitations. The first step is to make a choice, the second step is to support the choice, and the last step will issue success.

CHAPTER 1: LOVE THYSELF

One Life, One Opportunity and Many, Many Consequences

Life takes a toll on those who act before they think things through. Normally, we act then try to evade the consequences of our choices. Take the time to create a timetable to plan your success strategically throughout your life. Generate goals that contain a constant reminder that hard work enhances happiness. One of our greatest opportunities is the ability to try again, which so many of us take for granted. Once you open your eyes in the morning and inhale your first breath of a new day, smile. There is nothing that stands between you and peace of mind but yourself, your self-doubt, and your passive thoughts.

HELP!

Be Yourself or Become Selfless, Senseless and Soulless

One way to ridicule nature is by despising who you are. An individual is issued his own character, charisma, and confidence. Arrogance and insecurities are parasites that puncture the human pride. Who we are as individuals develops the society in which we dwell. Be willing to pardon because passion sometimes poisons people's perceptions. Be willing to understand because those who are perfect are nonexistent. Finally, be willing to endure and you will inherit knowledge, wisdom, and understanding. Who you were then should motivate who you are now to become the person you plan to be. First impressions capture the world's attention and focus it on your attitude. Your attitude will enter and exit doors that your physical make up will be denied. You have the power to justify who you are to the world by just being you.

CHAPTER 1: LOVE THYSELF

Independence Is the Courage to Stand Steadfast for What You Consider Correct

We live too much of our life striving to impress and please other people. Imagine being isolated from expectations and criticisms; picture a life filled with goals, purpose, and accomplishment. A wise individual goal is to live and praise God. You will never be able to live up to expectations that you did not envision for your own self. There is no one who knows your potential better than you do. Make sure you worship wisely because your Maker will provide all the independence that you pray for.

HELP!

I Am Only as Important to Myself as I Show Those Who Surround Me

Honor, respect, and trust begin with the first impression. If you do not command charisma from the start, people will form their own conclusions about who you are. Their opinions may damage your chances of getting to know someone new. An individual who only admires you will not last as long as the individual who loves you, but the one who respects you will last a lifetime. You can control those you deal with by having discipline and not changing direction when your emotions tempt you to detour from your path.

CHAPTER 1: LOVE THYSELF

They Said I Was a Horrible Human Being, and It Hurt Until I Chose to Be Humble

It is possible to become what you despise. If you are not secure and you allow pressure to sabotage your sanity, you may become passive. Then anger begins to bombard your thoughts, and your behavior becomes aggressive. The experience will either create character or sprinkle sorrow, which will eventually damage the soul. You will begin to heal once you take control of your emotions, which dictate how you handle life.

HELP!

Jealousy Jails the Individual Who Justifies His Displeasures with His Actions

Envy will eat away at your soul. Give yourself a harsh reality check to see the true you. It is not easy; the mind hides our faults from us. If you are willing to look upon your true self, you will not blame others for feeling dissatisfied. You will not grow angry and claim unfairness. Freedom from anger propels you to focus on your own personal goals and less on the accomplishments of others. Learn to condition yourself on the importance of self-evaluation because your own reality will set you free.

CHAPTER 1: LOVE THYSELF

I Refuse to Complain; the Reason I Am Upset Is Because I Am too Passive to Make a Change

Our mouth continues to lie as our actions display our honesty. Our unwillingness to address conflict tampers with our individual concerns. Our happiness suffers from our dedication to someone else's peace of mind. Our soul continues to waiver while our relationships continue to destroy our compassion. Our only chance to combat our ongoing epidemic is to be open and frank with ourselves.

Being Happy Can Become a Habit as Long as Being Miserable Can No Longer Be an Option

We cover our faults with attitude in an attempt to mask our choices. We deal with the first layer of personal issues in an effort to minimize the overall pain. If we spent quality time in correcting the internal image and not the physical one in the mirror, we would find ourselves in more healthy relationships. It is convenient to blame others and difficult to accept the anguish you have caused yourself and those close to you.

CHAPTER 1: LOVE THYSELF

A Leased Love Will Wind Up Lost, Lonely and Lifeless

A love based on material hugs and kisses will never survive a recession. People will tolerate your presence as long as you meet and exceed their list of needs. People will also utilize the pain you have shared to exploit compassion from your yearning heart. Lastly, people will leave a relationship that can no longer afford their affection. You cannot control people's motives, but you can control your currency. A true love will never come with a price tag. Learning to love begins with an investment allocated to you.

What Will You Do When Life as You Know It Fades Away?

A good life is taken for granted when you have given nothing to maintain happiness. A frown is one second away from becoming a tattoo smile on the face of a phony person. People will put up with your behavior until they decide that you are not their equal. Do not allow these types of people to use an angle to keep you at bay. You must realize relationships favor one party over the other at all times because most people will not reveal their agenda until the very end. Use your self-evaluation tools to gain self-awareness and push ignorance aside. You are only a fool when you continue to allow others to itemize your intentions and not theirs. We choose to rationalize in relationships rather than exit them expeditiously. After awhile we begin to question our own motives when the only answer is evident. Even when you think you are doing the right thing for others, sometimes it comes down to you having to leave to truly get their attention. Once you choose to leave, never look back, because sometimes leaving is the only consequence to make someone change for the better. They will only sincerely miss you when you have moved on to help someone else.

CHAPTER TWO

Where Do We Go From Here?

Chapter 2 offers a dream, destination, or destiny for the lost individual who has now come to terms with the extraordinary power of his or her inner strength. It is important to know who you are, but such knowledge is of no value, if you do not channel this newfound energy into purpose. Give your imagination reign during this second entry because previous self-imposed limitations distort our true desires. You have to believe nothing is out of your reach, and you are a choice away from any global position on this Earth. Close your eyes and allow your journey to take you to places you have been previously afraid to ask for. Now open your eyes and see the PATH of salvation, serenity, and success.

HELP!

Manipulate the Mainstream and the Rest Will Not Hesitate to Follow the Limelight

Pardon me, did you see which way I was supposed to go because I have made a wrong turn? I was going in the right direction until someone suggested I take a shortcut. I have been turned around before, but the destination was always navigated for me. I see a crowd, but they only move to the instruction of one individual, who is too busy to provide the answer for everyone. Finally, I see someone with charisma fielding questions from an obedient group. I knew plotting a map would be a waste of time, when everybody is going the same way I seem to be going. The world has silenced a smile and a handshake so watch traffic, if you have not researched the road ahead.

CHAPTER 2: WHERE DO WE GO FROM HERE?

For a Lifetime, I Have Survived by Word of Mouth

For a lifetime, I have survived by believing in anything other people said. For an eternity, I have lived life only by ear, listening to others without doing my own research. For the rest of my life, I will excel by using my hands—by putting pencil to pad to create a plan. Use your intelligence to plan and set goals—so that you can live and not just exist.

HELP!

I Love You Because I Love Me; I Hate You Because I Hate Me

Our actions are dictated by our personal views. We often judge and create stereotypes due to lack of confidence in our own abilities. We find comfort in the failures or struggles of others. This gives us a great deal of room for error. A reality check is not needed if these facts do not apply to you. The first step to recovery is to be 100 percent honest and view your own self for who you are.

CHAPTER 2: WHERE DO WE GO FROM HERE?

Are You Willing to Embrace the Past and Create a Contemporary You?

The mind creates obstacles that the body can not conquer. Have you stumbled in life for the last time and now wish to stand on solid ground? Are you fed up with your quality of life and now stand timid at the fork in the road? Fear will never allow freedom of expression or your ego to be grounded. It takes honesty to admit the error of our ways. Self-esteem allows us to be vulnerable and, at the same time, recognize our value. A plan is priceless when working toward goals in life. You are the only person keeping you from being where you want to be.

HELP!

I Can Do Nothing about Yesterday, But I Can Do Everything about Today

The only correction I can make at this point are the errors of my ways. I am now determined to display discipline to a detrimental existence. I imagine along the road of change you have to fall victim to weakness in order to enjoy a life of strength. Life is a choice within itself, and the majority of our decisions are pressure filled. Common sense is a majestic guide to life and the liberty of success. Plan ahead to become more efficient and to enjoy a more effective outcome. Do not hold back; give life your all and God will reward your effort with His grace, mercy, and blessings.

CHAPTER 2: WHERE DO WE GO FROM HERE?

The Locomotive Is Coming; What Do You Do?

Do you stand your ground and force derailment? Do you pull the lever and switch tracks to avoid the inevitable? The answer depends on the conductor's direction. What kind of conductor are you? The conveyance of life is ours to contrive, while we catapult intentions into certainty. During the course of change, we gather apprehension while on unfamiliar grounds. We must believe because going forward finalizes our fantasy ride. As we build momentum, we move memories to figments of our imagination to the next stop: the manifestation of conversion. To inherit our ideal allocation, we have to forfeit what's been good to us in our past, which allows room for abundance in the near future.

HELP!

Whether It's the Right or the Wrong Choice, the Circumstances Will Convey

Your reality depends on your individual courage to command options. You can follow instinct, impulse, or knowledge. Sometimes there are not enough hours in the day to collect adequate content to evaluate a carousel of fiction. Even with facts, our brilliance can be outwitted by the confidence of a fool—if we act on emotion. People often prefer to remain silent and allow someone else to set the agenda for their communities. It is your right to have a choice, even when you are afraid to take a chance and decide for yourself.

CHAPTER 2: WHERE DO WE GO FROM HERE?

The Past Is a Crutch That I Can Not Afford to Lean On

Some of us entwine our emotions in distant memories of the good old days. The rest of us entangle our emotions in the ambiguous acts of past failures. Either way, our fidelity should focus solely on our future and not on our self-imposed failure or fame. The present can not properly prepare for a future when your thoughts are fastened in the past. If we continue to move forward while looking backward, we will fall victim to surprise. As we struggle through our trying times, the information we are gathering through our experiences grooms our inner guidance for success. Devotion will display a real passion for a goal that has not been previously obtained. If you seek success without a plan, you will be stranded in quicksand. Plans are designed for the future, not the past.

HELP!

The Answer to the Addiction List

Men lust for women; women lust for men. Addicts lust for drugs, sex, food, alcohol, money, and the list goes on and on. How can we continue to be so selfish? There is nothing on God's green Earth that we should put before the Almighty. You should love nothing more than you love God. Let's get our lives in order!

CHAPTER 2: WHERE DO WE GO FROM HERE?

Your Dishonesty Humbles My Soul and Allows My Spirit to Be Even More Humble

Through the grace and mercy of God, I have pondered and realized it is not about an individual being dishonest; it's about me being more honest. We live in a world where we beat around the bush and shackle our tongues. We often withhold information or leave the most important part out on purpose, claiming that we do not want to hurt anyone's feelings. The longer you manipulate the truth, the more it will hurt the person you are lying to when they eventually figure you out. As children, we are exposed to the gray area of little white lies, and without careful gardening (a dedication to truth) that weed will bloom into a field of corruption. Little lies become big lies because once you tamper with the truth, the fairy tale begins and you have to make up an endless story as you go. Even if people do not appreciate the words you speak, blunt honesty demands respect. It takes true courage to stand for what's right and to speak against injustice.

Self-Reflection Allows a Moment to Reminisce or a Reason to Rectify Your Decision-Making Process

Being happy is the validation of life. We spend too much time muffled in misfortune. Shake yourself free. Focus on the favors that have been issued by God, even when you do not agree with the order of events God presents. Life is not as bad as we make it seem. The direction in which your life is headed stems from your own choices. When you reflect on past events, you must first be honest and, finally, humble. Do not prosecute the part of your life you have already witnessed; parole it. It is past; it is gone. There is no perfect person walking this Earth, no person who has not made mistakes, and no person who will not make mistakes in the future. So, do not set your goals to be dismissed. You should make every attempt to enjoy the here and now but make sure you establish a foundation for the future. We owe it to ourselves to reflect with an open mind and not justify our complaints.

CHAPTER 2: WHERE DO WE GO FROM HERE?

Common Sense Is the Logic That Fuels the Soul

A negative attitude occupies too much capacity in the mind. The flaws of others should not have any entertainment value. When we pay too much attention to the details concerning someone else, we are not paying interest in our own life. If you constantly are thinking negative thoughts about someone else, you can not concentrate on yourself. Focus on you and be good to yourself first; do not lose focus on your aspirations, your goals, and, most important, your own life. Peace and blessing to all.

HELP!

Wow! We Can See Someone's Faults a Mile Away, But Ours Remain a Mystery Only Inches in Front of Us

We abandon our own moral qualities when we question the morals of others but not ourselves. Be aware that jealousy alters what we really see. Do not waste time and effort on issues that keep you from exposing what's actual. We need to focus on what will better benefit the individual and dispose of gossiping because it hardly ever helps anyone involved.

CHAPTER 2: WHERE DO WE GO FROM HERE?

What Does the Company You Keep Say about the Person That You Are?

Do you take initiative and lead or do you flow with the herd? I believe there should be a universal standard of respect among people. A true leader is willing to die for his cause and his people. A leader can never exchange community success for personal gain. A leader is a position of high regard and a great deal of envy. You must make sure you screen the soldiers you recruit because one day you may have to go to war.

HELP!

How Humble Have You Been?

Cherish your companion and the company you keep. You can lead without overwhelming the people who are willing to follow. Orders are options that are better taken when issued with a choice. People will lift you no matter the weight once they believe, trust, and respect your direction. Do not lead when you are not willing to follow, and, most of all, humble your being.

CHAPTER 2: WHERE DO WE GO FROM HERE?

Neither Road Map, Compass Nor Navigational System Is of Any Value When the Blind Is Leading the Blind

When there is no sense of direction, everyone from leader to follower paces in a circle. Your foundation has to be built through God to remain intact through any groundbreaking event. The change begins within each individual who claims he or she is fed up with politics, racism, and the state of our society. At any given time, you can step out of the long line of followers and lead by example. Our society more than ever needs new leaders who are more than willing to blaze a trail.

HELP!

Education Is the Universal Language of Life, Liberty and Love

Knowledge has always opened doors that ignorance once held shut. The information highway has opened a carpool lane to enhance society's intellect. Libraries have always flooded the world with quality information and ideas. Malcolm X used the dictionary to free his mind and explore his wisdom. Education does not have to be validated by an academic degree, but a degree can demand respect. Research dictates the pace of the pupil who seeks to understand and learn from life. Every day God issues a lesson to each of us to continue our growth as individuals. We must keep in mind that it's not about how much information we can retain for ourselves. The goal is to share the information that you have embraced with the people around you, so we can all exercise our common sense.

CHAPTER 2: WHERE DO WE GO FROM HERE?

Pride Is a Flame That Burns Through Your Soul

It only requires a spark to ignite the fire. Explore your ethnicity, conquer your native culture, and investigate your place in history. History explains the distance we traveled as people. The road has been rough, but with the knowledge we've obtained from past experience, a bright future can be paved. It's your duty to know yourself, respect your elders, and live for your ancestors.

HELP!

Progress Begins When Each Individual Stands and Is Accounted For

Change begins with an action plan then a course of action. It does not take place with only complaints. We have allowed society to continue to disrespect, discriminate, and demolish our human race. We make the difference even as individuals who refuse to work toward the same agenda. We make a difference when we choose education and realize that all education should begin and end in the home. Our children should be our priority. We must offer additional education in the home, or we will continue to see our at-risk children in homes that contain bars. We have for far too long accepted an average education and blamed the system for lack of success. We all agree the odds are stacked against minorities, but education is the instant state lotto. You can not demand a fair shake; you have to command equal share. If you only bargain for crumbs, you will never negotiate enough flour to bake your own loaf of bread.

CHAPTER 2: WHERE DO WE GO FROM HERE?

Vote to Honor the Persistence of Our Patriarchs or Continue to Annihilate Their Struggle

Too many American citizens have been subjected to humiliation, hatred, and harm because of racism. Imagine the blatant denial of your basic human rights due to ethnicity. Fathom the abuse allocated for the minority man, woman, and child by the hypocrisy of America. Recall the tenacious torture endured by supporters of civil rights. A great many civilized citizens chose a nonviolent approach—as opposed to violent extremism—to an atrocious state of affairs. Voting eventually became the artillery to balance and undermine the persistent pressure of bigotry. Civil rights activists were able to withstand being hosed by water, struck by sticks, and plastered with saliva to secure their rights. The temperament of deprived individuals negotiated a treaty to command civil rights. We must capture the same spirit that willed souls for the quest of excellence. We can not remain passive in an aggressive society that preys on the humble. We must unite with our votes and display the pride that our patriarchs provoked.

HELP!

The Image, the Idea and the Reflection of Reality Isolates Insanity

What you see is not always what you get. If a coward displayed confidence, would you believe this to be a true characteristic? If you saw a brave individual humble himself to a crowd of cravens, would you doubt him in the next confrontation? If you took a glimpse of yourself during stress, strain, or even sacrifice, you would most likely not resemble the image in your mind. The person whom you assumed you would be has grown, and at first glance, you will not recognize what you have become. Your maturation may not be ideal, but sculpt the image in your mind and maintain reality as you manage sanity.

CHAPTER 2: WHERE DO WE GO FROM HERE?

What Action Will You Take in the Revolt?

Where will you stand when the war of words begins to destroy the enemy's target ? Are you willing to face the families of friendly fire when opinions begin to massacre emotions? Are you willing to sacrifice your reputation for your community and the future of young children? Are you willing to make a difference as a team player even if you must pawn your own glory? If not, remove yourself from the war room and allow room for a real role model. We must act now!

HELP!

Every Entity We Cherish in History Came Through the Womb of a Woman

I will do everything in my power to discontinue the disrespect, rape, and misconduct toward women (from the elderly to young girls). I will take full responsibility to set an example for my fellow men on how to respect, love, and appreciate our women. One woman is more than enough for one man.

CHAPTER 2: WHERE DO WE GO FROM HERE?

Success Seems Shallow
Suddenly Seconds Away

The wrong choice at the right moment will devastate any dream. The right person on a righteous path will rally the unjust. Those individuals who waiver will wake from weakness and celebrate strength. There are countless people who refuse to accept actions as the difference maker. The rest of us will wonder how talking about hard work was not enough to make a distinction. The cure will save the masses from an epidemic of excuses and allow accomplishment to alert us all.

CHAPTER THREE

God Help Us!

Chapter 3 introduces the importance of a faith-based balance between our choices and consequences. This third entry explores our belief system and the circumstances that force our hand to reach for forgiveness. The highest power of the universe has been issued titles to make each individual, group, or nation comfortable in commanding faith. Once you have established a sincere faith in yourself, you are allowed to worship without prejudice. You will learn that your connection is through your energy and not by opinion of mankind. You do not have to go through a spokesperson to redeem your deeds in the eyes of our Creator. You and your path have now been blessed by REDEMPTION. It is now your CHOICE to become who your wishes have always demanded YOU to be.

HELP!

I Have Hit Rock Bottom, But This Slide Symbolizes a Step in the Right Direction

It seemed like the bottom fell out of my existence, when everything was going so well. How could one impulsive choice at that one moment create a tailspin that would terrorize the days to follow? Pity has allowed me to create safeguards in being a victim of my own doing. My intentions were swamped by confusion, corruption, and carelessness. At the time, my conscious attempted to correct my behavior, but self-destructive tendencies had already affected my thoughts. The interest I pay daily for the pain I cost myself and others feels like a revolving rate. When I thought I was at my weakest, I had no choice but to weather the storm. During that time of sorrow, God's mercy ushered the clouds out of my life and delivered the sunshine that aided my growth.

CHAPTER 3: GOD HELP US

As Our Deeds Begin to Payoff, We Must Accept Account of the Dividends

We allow our ego to believe the good we receive in life is our doing, but somehow all the bad we encounter is never our fault. Judgment crosses the lips of liars and seldom saints. Everyone is not consumed by envy, but everything can, at times, not be enough for those who are stingy. The gift God gives is wrapped beautifully including a bow on the outside and a choice on the inside. Take all the energy you can generate and enjoy the favor of a free life.

HELP!

Do Not Allow Your Faith to Avalanche When the Struggle Is at Its Peak

A lifetime is a long time to live without any pressure or adversity. You must show gratitude when you have been showered with grace. Do not allow your ego to gloat when you have failed to issue our Supreme Being sufficient glory. The green valley will become the desert beneath the feet of an individual, who claims to have reached the apex alone.

CHAPTER 3: GOD HELP US

At Our Weakest Point, God Issues the Most Strength

Every man seems to have a breaking point, but at what point are you willing to die for your beliefs? If you soar through life with the expectations of others, you will crash and burn when you hit reality. Faith protects our passion, and praise sounds our cry for mercy. Integrity defends our soul from the detractions of wickedness. Our minds and bodies tend to tinker with dishonesty when we lust for the entertainment of this life. Only God can bless our beings with a balance that will blend with—but not give into—a corrupt society. Weakness is only a thought that delivers doubt to the conscious. Faith withstands all that is negative and detrimental to the spirit. Faith expands our thirst for wisdom, knowledge, and righteousness. God is always patient with the arrogant because He has the mercy to humble their nature. God is always present, but He only makes His presence known when we need Him the most.

HELP!

A Simple Second Can Salvage the Soul

Moments multiply into minutes as the masses are gridlocked by time. To unlock the genuine information highway, which is your mind, you have to caress the key of life. The hours in a day move at such a rapid pace that tomorrow seems to come before today. We all reflect on the journey time has imposed on our lives. Time will puzzle you because God assembles life in pieces. Time seems to move slowly until you realize a section of your life has already passed. Time is the tactic God uses to sober our souls. The soul is parallel to the portal of flesh we enter leaving the womb. We only maintain a slim chance of survival by the structure we receive from our parents; the world has the odds stacked against a pure person of faith. Society has cloned mental slavery and injected it into lost souls. God waits patiently for us to go down on bended knee to repent for our salivation. A great many of us now travel through life living on a second chance. Do not take any of your seconds of breath for granted. We all must take a second out of each day and give praise to the Creator of us all.

CHAPTER 3: GOD HELP US

I Do Not Have to Justify Who I Am or Who I Worship to Anyone; God Loves Me Anyway

We spend more energy battering fellow religions than we do studying the text that holds the key to our salvation. The actual doctrines provoke peace and a palace of serenity in our souls. Our judgments toward our peers are immoral, invalid, and unjust. Life is not ours to ridicule or to remove from existence. Embrace and enjoy the company God has sent to mingle with us. God's color contrast is Neapolitan to the eyes of man. Good or evil knows no color. Only the individual heart will shine shades through the soul. We maintain a mask to marvel mankind, but God can see through the masquerade. If we would only ask for mercy, our Savior's forgiveness is genuine and not to be confused with grudges held by men. My Savior salutes me, while men sanction my every step. My Lord loves me, while men attempt to limit my life. My God grants me beauty and abundance, while men attempt to garnish the growth of my grace. I will only look to perfection for my guidance, and I will allow men to be only men.

HELP!

God Anchors the Soul to Save the Fragile Flesh

Temptation tames and tinkers our conscious to waiver willpower. Sin seduces. Faith once realized can ration the rules of one's life. Why would the flesh wish to continue a war when it is its own enemy and the spirit has been blessed with a suit of armor? The soul may lapse, but the spirit inserts longevity when the flesh returns to dust. The flesh promotes panic and penalizes the soul for its follies. Karma is exposed to the mind, body, and soul through the revelation of our actions. The detrimental deeds of the past can doom the days of tomorrow. Repent to repair all bridges that your path has damaged during the course of your life. Allow nature to nestle life and enjoy the breeze of being blessed. The flesh is controlled by the faith when individuals return to their Maker.

CHAPTER 3: GOD HELP US

Has Man Removed Facts from Religion or Has Religion Ridiculed Man?

Do you allow your faith to be tormented in religious practices? Does the word of God stand the test of time in a corrupt person's mind? Will the pulpit continue to make promises that it can not keep? Faith is the perception of an individual's personal opinion, belief, and point of view toward God. Do not allow your faith to be dictated by the thoughts of perverse people. Allow your conscious to decipher the differences denominations make in the same belief. All religions seem to have the same prophets, and they all seem to manifest an original tale. I believe there is only one God, and He has allowed several paths back to His glory. For the sake and salvation of yourself, pick your path and begin your pilgrimage.

HELP!

Parity Pleases Our Creator, But Man Continues to Make Excuses for Greed

Life is fair through the eyes of the Lord. Man's calculation has made our country's currency difficult to balance. Passive people are pushed aside because the American pie has been sliced with a chainsaw. The gift you give may be the charity that harvests the hope of the next individual. A selfish soul loses sight of sound judgment and problem solving. Society can afford a smorgasbord to feed us all; however, we hoard and allow humans to starve. Where is our sense of equality for fellow families, friends, and even foes? Love seems to lose steam the moment people can no longer do what we demand. The culture in which we're raised can command a limited outlook on life. The world has a variety of flavors, and we have lost our sense of taste. Being gentle gains admiration from the group of humble human beings that gather just to be around your bountiful behavior. Many human beings offer no compassion when it comes to livelihood of the next human. Faith will bring the blessing we need to combat covetousness.

CHAPTER 3: GOD HELP US

There Is No Blemish Any Attack Can Bestow, Once You Are in Tune with Your Testimony

Once you choose to plant your feet in the soil of faith, forever is not long enough to retain feelings of fear.

HELP!

Everything Is Never Enough, When Your Eyes Are Filled with Tears of Greed

Everyone around you can see the joy of your environment, but you complain anyway. The sight of your success suggests to strangers that you have to be blind to blaspheme these blessings. Your vision has altered to the degree that you tangle the truth to transpose what's rationale to you. You claim to want more, you demand independence, but you do nothing to secure this farfetched fantasy. When you only take and you seldom give, you will continue to be forsaken from seeing the true meaning of alms.

CHAPTER 3: GOD HELP US

The Word of God Is Translated Through the Sins of Mankind

Our trials and errors serve as a warning to the clones of our ways. Our Creator has allowed a clear conscious to settle our mischievous thoughts and immoral behavior. There is a constant contrast of what's right against the temptations of this world. We continue to navigate upstream in the Nile of lust looking for the land of leisure. We also continue to multiply our sins allowing each sin to surpass the last sin. Consequence speaks softly to our conscious as a reminder to control our character. The temptation of the supreme spirit of evil speaks shrewdly to manipulate our minds in a malicious way. It is up to the individual to tip the scale to the side of serenity and relinquish sin.

HELP!

Why Do We Exploit Each Other? Why Are the Principles of Religion We Speak of So Difficult to Live?

We utilize Third World countries to produce our goods at the cost of bankrupting our own citizens. We pay pennies for labor and make millions in revenue. The urban community sponsors these non-United States factories with loyal support. The goal of profit keeps these same corporations out of East Saint Louis, Harlem, and Watts. Being Christian, Jewish, Jehovah Witness, or Muslim does not excuse the poverty of poor judgment. God imbedded the thoughts of compassion in our mind and the strands of solace in our heart. Ultimately, the choice is yours, but keep in mind your day will come to pay the debt of your deeds.

CHAPTER 3: GOD HELP US

Our Mentality Has Become Mute to Madness; Society Has Allowed an Evil Being to Work Its Black Magic

The world is at war, and our souls are at stake. Molesters are abusing minors, man's greed has raped the economy, and evil seems to rule the Earth. Hollywood has spared no expense to display the destruction of the world for entertainment value. Human beings have made great strides in the attempt to bust through the ozone layer. The rain forest will soon be a desert if man continues to destroy our green Earth. God chose to use the penis and the womb as a way to reproduce life, but man has spread death (AIDS) through unprotected intercourse. The demons of the world continue to destroy, devastate, and dictate the opportunities of life. Faith is now in an awkward position, but the positive energy of the universe issues faith a fighting chance to knock out evil.

HELP!

The Value of Life Continues to Decline and the Afflicted Families Are in a State of Depression

Death looks upon society and smiles at our continued effort to rid the Earth of life. Murder mingles with greed, envy, and hypocrisy to endorse hate. Conflict seems to lead to wars because ego will not allow another's opinion. We are losing life to the armed forces because poor people have limited liberties. We are also losing life to drugs and alcohol because poor people are looking to escape misery and entertain paradise. In conclusion, we are losing life to senseless violence in urban America because we have been conditioned to hate who we are as people. If there were sincere limits levied on gun manufacturers, life would not be so easy to take in a fit of rage. There are no so-called gangs, thugs, or criminals in the urban community that manufacture mass weapons of destruction. Weapons are big business, and we live in a society that cherishes and profits from firearms. We should not be caught off guard by the alarming high murder rate that increases each year in this nation. Dinosaurs and cavemen are extinct, and if we do not begin to value life, so will be human beings.

CHAPTER 3: GOD HELP US

Life Is Seldom What It Seems; Do Not Be Fooled By an Illusion

Just because you see a person smile that does not guarantee that they are happy. We walk through life adapting to the ways of the world. Followers favor friends who have no leadership appeal. Why do so many allow their ego to soar with arrogance and then maintain minimum self-esteem? Too many individuals claim to be experts, flooded with experience but often falling victim to pressure. Why do we consider a detrimental relationship to be filled with love? Why does a lesson have to be fatal before we will accept the same information by ear? Why do we continue to disobey the authority of our Almighty, when the Day of Judgment may be near?

HELP!

Each Child Should Begin with Its Own Angel, But God Will Allow an Angel to Anoint Another Child to Share His Own

The deed of donation is an exciting energy that fuels the soul. There is no feeling in the world like the sentiment of giving without attachments. Even those who have an ulterior motive, when they issue without a cause, will find the gratitude of the impoverished humbling. We have more than enough resources to rectify the poverty crisis in this world and the next to follow. Give plenty, and when you do share your wealth, give from the heart.

CHAPTER 3: GOD HELP US

There Can Stand One Million Men Between You and Your Faith

Each man can be obnoxiously opposed to what you know in your veins to be true. Still you stand. The only alliance you need is the one with God. The whole world can stand against you, but that is nothing compared to God being within you. It seems nothing matters to us unless it happened to us. A day should not pass that we do not stand diligent for truth and equality. Serenity and justice should be imperative not preference.

Where Will Your Faith Lie? Good or the Root of All Evil?

In God we trust, even American currency notes this fact. God has allowed a choice among men. What road will you take to navigate salvation? What direction will you offer to help others lost on their way to heaven? When will you decide to change your life and live for grace, gratitude, and a higher greatness? The dollar will come and go as long you spend the dollar that you do not have. One dollar will become a rare two dollar bill if you choose to share your last legal tender.

CHAPTER FOUR

Faith, Dreams and Aspirations

Chapter 4 suggests you select a challenge that initiates conflict with meritocracy. This is your opportunity to explore which avenue aligns your aspirations. You now have to compile all your what-ifs into one daydream and create your field of dreams. In the beginning, you will have to make-believe, but when faith reconciles your course of action, the results are all yours to cherish. Faith allows just enough belief to believe in the unseen, unknown, and unfulfilled opportunities of the universe. This fourth entry allows dreams and aspirations access to the core of our expectations of self. It is magical—once you get in tune with who you are, where you are going, the support of salivation and doing whatever your FAITH, DREAMS, and ASPIRATIONS have dictated. Happiness is no longer hindered by you, but you will now see clearly those who are not happy for your new appreciation of YOUR LIFE!

HELP!

I Sit Back and Smile and the Happiness Hollows My Soul

No matter how harsh you perceive life to be, someone somewhere has it harder than you. Our serenity starts with the attitude that we allow the world to see. People normally react to the personality that they encounter. People are more responsive to kindness than arrogance. A smile, a gentle hello, or a kind word can help return joy to an individual who is troubled. A shun, a sarcastic stare, or showboating can lead to animosity. We each have the power to embrace the evolution and educate our ignorant. I see too many of us who are afraid to ask for help and too many of us who refuse to give aid to anyone. A small donation of emotion and passion will grace our globe, if we all gather together for the purpose of prosperity. Do your part. Inspire the Earth to rejoice, redeem, and rid itself of sorrow.

CHAPTER 4: FAITH DREAMS AND ASPIRATIONS

Opportunity's Door Only Opens a Split Second, So Move Swiftly to Secure Your Space

I am everything that I sacrifice to be. I will not be deterred from my goals by the limitations of society. I will create a momentum that will mesmerize the individuals who may doubt me. I will use nonviolence filled with vigor to maintain my emotions when verbally attacked. I will not give an inkling of ignorance, and I will demonstrate a calm that can not be tested. I will be an advocate for all and remain selfless for those who continue to admire me. I will multiply this one chance into equality that has created a new commander-in-chief.

HELP!

Seconds Grow into Moments and Eventually One Day Blossom into Being a Choice!

The gamble we take with our daily lives is we will wake up the next morning. Many of us move through our existence in slow motion, choosing not to challenge our lives with goals and objectives. Some of us, who are a little more active, set safe goals that we know will not challenge our being in the least. Those individuals continue to succeed in life but not in happiness. The rest of us challenge ourselves and society because the goals we set seem to change the world; such people are aggressive and do not take no for an answer. These people enjoy the most success as well as the most failure because they took a massive chance in the first place. Now, the question is: Which one are you? You may want to be a combination of all three because moving too slowly, just moving along, and moving too fast are all needed to survive in this society.

CHAPTER 4: FAITH DREAMS AND ASPIRATIONS

A Dream Will Dare Diligence to Dominate

The mind hopes success crosses our path. The body wishes extra weight away. The soul prays that the spirit will be saved. All these are dreams until action begins to make choices practical. You are foolish to believe life offers anything for free. Act now. Blood, sweat, and tears are the payment for the gift of daydreaming.

Faith! Do You Have Confidence in Your Ability?

Liberate your mind, body, and soul by investing action into your dreams. Free your mind and allow your aspirations to run wild in endangered wilderness. Explore your thought processes for all the things you like to do or things that you are excellent at doing. Set a goal to achieve the most popular idea you can create and command success while you go for it. For example, go back to school to acquire your education, go to the gym to lose forty-five pounds, or open up your own successful business. Our aspirations love the vision of our faith and dreams entangled in diligence.

CHAPTER 4: FAITH DREAMS AND ASPIRATIONS

Without Focus, an Individual Will Continue to Fall Short, Falter and Fail

A goal truly yearned for will always keep you honest. When want and need mesh together, determination will lead the way to success. Bliss is always hampered by procrastination because time can be sensitive. Preparation will keep you from living on a stopwatch. There is a sincere sense of enjoyment when you begin to reap the results of a passion-filled achievement. You can drastically enhance your quality of life, if you only envision the potential you have yet to fulfill. The heavens are the limits for each soul that begins and ends each day in faith. Faith is the tool God hands us to fix any problem or complete any project. The only barrier between you and anything you wish for is the lack of belief we all cherish.

HELP!

We Must Find a Way to Exceed All Limits

We all wish for the American dream, but the majority of us continues to live the American nightmare. You are who you wish, but you will be what you sacrifice to become. There is no quick way to obtain or escape life's experience and priceless preparations. You have to accept the information that's readily available and be willing to seek out the truth if necessary. You also have to be ready to decipher fact and fiction while communicating contrast. If you exercise the good sense you were born with and refuse to listen to second hand rhetoric, you will be able to recognize reality. Your own personal path will be filled with struggles but that is the point where you will persevere or give in to adversity. Struggle enhances your thoughts, talents, and temper. Embrace life and the good and bad times will balance themselves out.

CHAPTER 4: FAITH DREAMS AND ASPIRATIONS

The Day You Wait for Help Will Be the Day Life Passes You By

A helping hand should only handle a small portion of your own personal responsibilities. The average person will take kindness and compassion out of context until the giver perceives their grace as being weak. Asking for aid should never be the sole answer to your problem. Tend to your own business as much as possible. Do not allow those who choose to assist you to handicap your ability to get your chores done. Even the Good Book explains, as per the Creator, the law of the land is to help those who help themselves. I choose independence, taking control of my destiny and not allowing anyone to let me down in the process.

HELP!

Sacrifice Sets the Standard for Dreams, Goals and Self-Preservation

Only in fiction does a man or a woman stumble onto a pot of gold at the end of the rainbow. Few people inherit fortunes, and even fewer are lucky enough to hit the lotto. Most of us must figure a way through a nine-to-five to manhandle an economy that is manipulated by greed. We have to balance here and now to envision a future worth its weight in gold. A genuine effort evolves into an attitude that surmounts all desired needs and wants. Aspirations allow you to attack self-imposed boundaries and believe in your own ability. Willpower will help stop the spread of struggle to the subconscious. The power of belief and a firm stance in faith will lead you to the sweet taste of success. There is nothing to lose if you wake up today and secure a solid foundation for tomorrow.

CHAPTER 4: FAITH DREAMS AND ASPIRATIONS

It Was Not Over; I Chose to Quit Before My Perseverance Could Prevail

No matter what the odds or obstacles, you must believe in your ability. You have to will yourself to overcome emotion, when it seems there are no logical reasons left to achieve this individual accomplishment. The fight that you have left must overpower the fear that you have left. The win will offer the opportunity to overcome, overshadow, and oppress your last lost. A cheater is willing to win at any cost, but hard work has always bankrupted sore losers. You will only be what you have dedicated yourself to desire.

HELP!

Change Breeds Fear

The initial reaction to an idea that seems out of the ordinary often is criticism and opposition. Individuals with these ideas must believe vigorously in their ideas, to the point that they constantly visualize the outcome. We are afraid of anybody who selects success before us and is willing to sacrifice to succeed. People panic then become paranoid because they were not prepared for change. If you waiver once you recognize your own reflection, the sight of anybody else's shadow will startle you.

CHAPTER 4: FAITH DREAMS AND ASPIRATIONS

Karma Spins Out of Control But Always Seems to Stay on Course

Why? asks the individual in misery. Why not? answers life. Justice demands that all debts be paid on time. The law of nature refuses to be cheated. Our Commander-in-chief (the most high) allows consequences to the choices that we make. The nature of man dictates the spirit of the heart. We must hold a moral regard for all people we meet. The value of respect pays off tremendous dividends. Your attitude is the key to opening any door you wish to enter or exit.

HELP!

Do Not Wonder, Waiver, or Ask Why Because the Sphere Has Adjusted Its Axis to Allow Abundance in Your Forecast

Being nervous will negate the necessities when you partially believe in a well-known agenda. Once you hesitate to accept accurate data, doubt will damage belief in the process. The truth is silent against lies, believing clarity will weed out commotion. Comprehension cancels consideration of uncivilized thoughts that spread cancer to our conscious. The alpha of acknowledgement lies in the concern of the conflict and not in the omega of being obligated. It is possible your dream will be answered after the first slumber, or it may take an entire night of rest, or even years in a self-induced coma. Do not wonder, waiver, or ask why. Belief will continue to combat hallucination along the way.

CHAPTER 4: FAITH DREAMS AND ASPIRATIONS

A New Beginning Can Begin Today, a New Beginning Will Begin Today, a New Beginning Has Begun!

There is no limit to starting over and giving your life a second chance. You may need multiple opportunities to get your life going in the right direction so do not give up prematurely. You are only in a race against yourself because your enjoyment of life is at stake and no one else's. We will all fall short at times, but the difference in success and failure is the recovery time. Do not give up on your greatness, just because you find energy to expedite everyone else's agenda. Condition yourself to remember how important your desires are and pursue them to the smallest detail. What extreme are you willing to challenge yourself to capture ultimate serenity?

HELP!

We Have Been Blessed with a Drum That Beats Beautifully in Our Soul

An individual's life is similar to an orchestra. You have several instruments, all in tune, in an attempt to create a symphony. Life is like a melody that never ends, and you are the composer. We sometimes sing off-key and miss a note, but our soul will balance the eloquent sound of success. We have to expand our imagination and develop an ear for bliss because, just like music, life is filled with distortion and has to be equalized.

CHAPTER 4: FAITH DREAMS AND ASPIRATIONS

Cherish the Blessing of a Child

God designates parents as He sees fit. The passion a mother provides for a son or the protection a father will forever feel for a daughter is as fascinating as life itself. Do not allow yourself to think of your blessing as a burden. It's your job to instill love, morals, and self-esteem into your child so the outside world won't have 100 percent influence on your child's psyche. Children believe there are no boundaries or limits in their audacious world. The only limitations a child invests in are the boundaries you sell them. Do not sell your child short of all the wonderful avenues life has to offer. It is a progenitor's duty to help his or her offspring tap into all the potential their minds, bodies, and souls can imagine.

HELP!

Love Is the Cure for Lost Souls

An innovation of faith, peace, and serenity begins with a reality check. How honest have you been with your own self? If you refuse to critique your well-being, who are you to pass judgment on the next hypocrite? The most important love in the world is faith in God and the security of self. It seems to me society has allowed hate to hail love and destroy the passion people possess. Do we even honor our Bibles, Qurans, or Torahs? The text of God teaches from many different angles, and we even find fault in faith. God placed a compass within each of us to return to His grace. The turbulence of our journey is balanced by our behavior. Faith is the beam that holds the structure of life in position. The healing of lost souls begins and ends with genuine love for self.

CHAPTER 4: FAITH DREAMS AND ASPIRATIONS

Father Time Stands Timid in the Presence of Love

There is no distance too far to seek the companionship of a potential soul mate. There is no distance that could ever destroy the desire of destiny. There is no distance between us because I keep you in mind with a vivid vision. I now know a childhood crush can evolve into love at first sight when you never realize the true value of a one-of-kind relationship. In my wildest dreams, I never imagined these feelings for an old friend would flow with so much passion. Being blessed to see you after all these years has allowed time to stand silent for a moment. I am a man today, and I have the pleasure of seeing the woman you have worked so hard to become. Men and women have both entered and exited our lives, but today brings us back together and if it was only for that second, I now know that I am in love with you.

HELP!

Adversity Is in the Mind

Prosperity pours slowly into a pool of life. Hard work delivers a charity of success in a selfish world. Life is not filled with luck, chance, or coincidence. Sacrifice can shoulder the burden of dreams and goals. A plan is a servant to willpower and dictates the attack on limitations. Pain is only a short inconvenience compared to the endless joy of the soul. Quitting is the quickest way to embrace failure and establish low self-esteem. Our mind creates all struggles that we encounter, so there is no reason not to figure your way through them intelligently.

CHAPTER 4: FAITH DREAMS AND ASPIRATIONS

Financial Success and Security Begin When You Own Your Own Path

A prosperous path is paved in ownership and monetary freedom. Sacrifice sends a clear message to the future that you mean business and prepare for fortune. Inflation ignites the greed of the wicked and repossesses the currency of poor people. Peace of mind is expensive in today's society. Some souls seem to come cheap when there is no food on the table. When you only lease employment, your livelihood is in the grip of another man. There are no get-rich-quick schemes because the dollar has become too competitive to obtain. There are no guarantees in business so do not fall victim to fool's gold and greed. Faith reminds man not to be blinded by the root of all evil. Success is sparked by word of mouth and the ability to network. You do not have to have all the money in the world to be happy and content with your own success.

HELP!

What Is Wealth without a Person to Share the Passion?

A sensuous soul mate is the desire of any lover. Even the Good Book explains that woman was created from the rib of a man. Life evolves dramatically when there is someone who brings constant joy. Butterflies boil in the heat of our stomach in the presence of a sincere companion. It takes a distinctive individual to erupt emotion and happiness that has been concealed overtime. An ardent lover is generated by faith and the ability to recognize a genuine person. Cherish the moment of love because all soul mates do not last a lifetime. Celebrate and rejoice in the bosom of love with poise and understand the passion that you bring to someone's heart. Love is solace when the spirit blends with the soul of someone special. God will reveal the love of your life when you feast in faith and embrace patience with open arms.

CHAPTER 4: FAITH DREAMS AND ASPIRATIONS

Success Is a Journey Not a Destination

Life consists of door one, door two, and door three. Which do you open to find your way back to God? Strive in life to be an honest, humble, and happy human being. That is the door to God.

HELP!

Paradise Is Plentiful

Imagine a day that begins with excellence and ends with ecstasy. In a liberated life, your mind visualizes your journey before you actually take a step. Your venture demands discipline to get results and a mind that does not entertain envy but only its own ideas. I believe everyone is entitled to abundance; they only need to choose to challenge their capabilities and ponder the principles that lead to the pinnacle of their desires.

CHAPTER FIVE

The Blues!
(Constructive Criticism)

Chapter 5 commands that you remain respectful against all agents of doubt and accept reality for what it is—not what suits our personal agenda or personality. Honesty erupts emotions that evolve from dishonesty. This fifth entry will dare you to speak through your deeds, but the translation may expose the contrast between your words and actions. It is difficult to accept our actions when faced with attitude, but karma claims countless concessions. "The Blues" is intended to motivate our maturation and mimic a self-imposed reality check, which allows a reflection of our growth. You will also learn the difference between an individual's opinion and constructive criticism. You are now prepared to remain humble against persecutions and are equipped to persevere against all obstacles.

HELP!

There Is a Reason Behind Each Action, Even When It Seems There Is No Logic

We all wonder why others act the way they do. I believe, at the time, most of us consider our choices to be correct and precise. Problems begin when we choose to act before we thoroughly think things through. This is not always the best scenario when pressure tends to force out focus. We mingle with mishaps because we are accustomed to flirting with failure. Even worse, some seem to enjoy the gamble of life and do not flinch when the stakes are detrimental. Negative outcome seems to surprise the individual who chooses to dance with the devil. Reality dissolves the fabric that covers up lies and deceit. Poor preparation establishes a weak link that evolves into a chain reaction of bad behavior.

CHAPTER 5: THE BLUES (CONSTRUCTIVE CRITICISM)

The Mind Will Make Sense to Our Perplexed Psyche

I have an aphorism that I swear by: "People will make it make sense to themselves." There is no right or wrong because our consciousness defends our opinion. When you pour intelligence into a lost soul, you get a genius without moral manners. If an imbecile is guided by the information of a scholar, his brilliance will birth a savant. The mind is a gift; if you share it, the surprise will startle you.

HELP!

'The Truth Hurts' Is a Cliché That Dishonest People Use to Avoid Honesty

The truth is stern; it stings and it leaves a stain on anything it comes in contact with. The truth is a bully that bothers those who tell little white lies; it nags habitual liars. The truth is an honest being whom dishonest people refuse to socialize with.

CHAPTER 5: THE BLUES
(CONSTRUCTIVE CRITICISM)

The Hour Glass Doesn't Pause So Manage Your Time

A child imagines the day he becomes an adult. An adult misses the days of childhood when responsibility was hardly a thought in the day and outcomes did not weigh so heavily. The elderly want to be young again, while their bodies dictate that they grow old. You will never be exactly where you want to be in life, but you can plan, prepare, and conceive your next crowning accomplishment. It would be wise to manage your time because you only have the option to review the choices you have made. Life does not offer the luxury to rewind, erase, and redo the actions that alter your state of being. A child has hope, an adult has consequences, and the elderly have regrets if they wasted too much time in their lives.

HELP!

Going Through the Motions Doesn't Precipitate Progress

Goals are elusive when we put forth a slumber effort. Our goals are grouped together with our everyday life and the unexpectedness that goes with it. Goals are the visions we view before we seek our desires. It takes discipline to motivate maturity that will maintain courage, compassion, and charisma. Honest habits sets the tone for success, while dedication dilutes the chance of botching up the job. Earnest effort combats the lack of willingness to work diligently toward a task. Adversity teases the character and provides passion to propel through hard times. Some goals are difficult to grasp but are worth the grit and grind once you've gained success. True success comes easily once you prepare for the worst and embrace excellence.

CHAPTER 5: THE BLUES
(CONSTRUCTIVE CRITICISM)

Where Will You Be When There Is Someone in Need?

Do you allow the selfishness in you to shut out the world? Do you demand aid when you are in need and forget to offer a hand when you see someone else in distress? Does your whole vocabulary consist of me, myself, and I? Do you judge someone's character before you sympathize with their situation? Does your attitude by-pass concern for the next individual's safety? Has a selfish society poisoned your perception of people's problems? We have been influenced to avoid unity and only concentrate on self-preservation. As long as American citizens live as individuals, society will always dictate our status as human beings. Religion commands that you want for your neighbor as you wish for yourself. We all may choose a different name for God, but we all must forgive and follow the mercy of our Master, who insists we help the individual in need.

HELP!

If You Refuse to Remove Your Hands from Your Pockets, I Can not Continue to Extend My Hand without Recourse

You do not seek a helping hand; you want a handout. Your plan and premise is to collect on favors; you believe you are entitled or owed. You have gouged out the goodness in those who surround you and sabotaged the safety net that has held you. You are finally on your own, and the independence you demand has demolished you. Now, you are forced to see the real you, the person who created these complications.

CHAPTER 5: THE BLUES
(CONSTRUCTIVE CRITICISM)

Emotional Buying Will Bankrupt You

The balance between needs and wants is separated by the weight of turmoil. The tags that tailor the wardrobe and the labels that lace designer shoes escort security out of our life. Consider the value of trinkets. Compliments inspired by envy make us feel empowered. But what is the price of that feeling? Responsibility has to revoke privileges that are detrimental to future investments. If an entire economy can fall victim to its own greed, then one vulnerable individual does not stand a chance against debt.

HELP!

Debt Shackles the Ability to Invest Freely In Our Future

Debt is a financial form of slavery. When you are in debt, you often live paycheck to paycheck, never really getting ahead. Let's look at some basic economics. Credit cards will eat up your capital and dig a financial hole so big a giant could not climb out of it. High interest rates are the chains and whips used to keep society in debt. Our government can not balance the nation's budget, so why would it be interested in your balanced budget? Credit cards are issued to hustle the consumer to purchase all the things we think we can afford. Foolish consumers are the victims of a system that loots poor people of their revenue. The interest rates to the rich are low because if they borrow a dollar, they can afford to pay back a dollar (thus avoiding the accumulation of interest). The same dollar that is borrowed by the poor may have the same interest rate, but it costs the poor so much more. They can't pay back that dollar so quickly and often end up paying much more than what they originally owed. Our society has to discontinue the misuse of power and exercise some morals to gain control of greed.

CHAPTER 5: THE BLUES
(CONSTRUCTIVE CRITICISM)

Hard Work Is Picking Cotton from Dusk to Dawn for Pennies, Sewing Fabric in a Sweatshop from Sun Up to Sun Down for Nickels

Please make sure you count your blessings. Our world has made slaves of men, women, and children for profit. Human dignity and culture have been stripped due to greed. Take a moment and ponder: Is flipping burgers for minimum wage as you work your way through college really that bad?

HELP!

God Blesses the Day of Our Birth

We leave the womb innocent and pure and enter a world of parasites. A child is not born a racist, rapist, or killer. Our society creates these people. It has created hell on Earth. Narrow-minded adults brainwash their children, filling them with a negative view of life. Then they go out into the world and spread that negativity. This Earth will never see peace until we change the arrogance in our souls.

CHAPTER 5: THE BLUES
(CONSTRUCTIVE CRITICISM)

God Has Blessed Us with a Personal Temple. Do You Take Pride in the Maintenance of Your Body?

You do not have to be on a health kick to live and eat right. It is a good idea to monitor the food that you put into your body. If peace of mind is your ultimate destination, then a healthy body is required for the journey.

HELP!

Our Future Will Continue to Crumble as Long as We Corrupt, Cheat and Castrate Our Children's Information and Intellect

Society has made a mockery of the importance of education. Today's curriculum has cleared the path to illiteracy. An uneducated child with exceptional talents will be ravished as an adult by a system that takes advantage of the foolish. Education has evaporated, while crime has become more ubiquitous. Lack of education and criminal behavior only lead to a life of trials and life sentences. Education begins in the home, continues in school, and expands through personal development, life experience, and religion.

CHAPTER 5: THE BLUES
(CONSTRUCTIVE CRITICISM)

A Man's Maturity Is Advertised by Action, Not Words

When we embrace one of life's lessons, we mature in the process. We seem to never reach the peak of mental capacity even though we believe we know it all. God has a way of reminding you of your position in life and the strides you have failed to take. A swift tongue can slow your forward progress by not being humble. Words have a way, if not chosen carefully, to come back and stalk you. Communication can cause heartache. Mature individuals live in balance and are not swayed by emotions. Faith secures maturity. We as mature adults must clip the wings of our ego to invest quality in an arrogant society.

HELP!

Refusing to Admit Flaws Keeps Us from Hearing Our True Music

The tone of honesty is not audible to all. We all have flaws, but many of us refuse to own our imperfections. Often it is not until we are challenged with the facts that we face them. And then our bluster and lies and excuses must fall silent. A wolf pack being misled by a sheep in wolf's clothing shall display no mercy when true nature calls to howl at a full moon. A character defect dims the demeanor and hides in denial. A person who continues to orchestrate a band filled with false notes will eventually compose the blues. If you can not read the notes, you will be forced to face the music from the true director.

CHAPTER 5: THE BLUES
(CONSTRUCTIVE CRITICISM)

The Weight I Chauffeur Continues to Drive Away Opportunities Because the Road Is Filled with Breakdowns

I am overweight, but there is more to it than the pounds I have packed on. I am a slum lord when it comes to my weight management, health, and temple. I am not hungry, but I continue to eat anyway due to stress I am not addressing. My heart will give out eventually or the weight of the stress will lead to a stroke. I will allow the high blood pressure to drown me because the side affects of the medicine make me feel like I'm running in quicksand. I gain weight by pounds but seem to be only able to lose by quarter pounds. I will not lose this weight until I stop losing my mind.

HELP!

Experience Is the Best Teacher; There Is No Right or Wrong Way to Become a Better Person

If you never fall short, you will never realize there is room for correction. Utilize your mistakes as a carriage to the palace of life. The rewards life offers are in reach if you only stand up and raise your hand. God does not enjoy the pain we seek; we choose to put ourselves in positions that are not healthy, safe, or wise. It is up to you to make sound and reasonable decisions. Every time you enter a fork in the road, grow from the outcome, be it good or be it not so good.

CHAPTER 5: THE BLUES (CONSTRUCTIVE CRITICISM)

Everybody Seems to Have an Opinion

What makes a thought valid? I believe a person's motive will decide the validity of his thoughts. Do you believe in human rights? Do you believe all men are created equal? Does racism exist in your world? What role does God play in your life? Now ask yourself do you have a valid opinion?

HELP!

Do Not Allow Your Companion to Hold Your Happiness Hostage

You relinquish your power once your joy is dictated by someone else. As long as you're content with your pace in life, your goals will be the only push you'll need. All the support, comfort, and serenity you seek from man can only be found in God. Do not allow the emotional stress of others to be an anchor around your throat. Your growth as a person will only peak when your ego returns from flight.

CHAPTER 5: THE BLUES
(CONSTRUCTIVE CRITICISM)

Karma Will Always Return to the Sender with or without Postage

What goes around will come back around, or as the Good Book explains: "As you sow, so shall you reap." God allows life to be as fair as you make it. If you thrive on negative situations, you will always find yourself a star in your own drama. Life is what you make it; if you do not offer anything, you will not receive anything. If you offer heart, humility, and honesty, you will receive everything your dreams desire.

CHAPTER SIX

Wherewithal (By Any Means Necessary)

Chapter 6 establishes equality for everyone and presents the step-by-step side effects of the lack of equality for all human beings in a barbaric society. Wherewithal would best describe the courage commanded in this extraordinary chapter? This sixth entry is based on an inner strength, personal desire, and destiny. It takes a group of sincere individuals to forgive those who forsake their basic human needs and rights by the law of the land. The will of an individual will outlast the hatred of an individual because positive energy will forever highlight the punishment of our past experience. When a people have experienced the worst treatment possible and still persevered through the pain and passion of their ancestors, they are a chosen and humble group of people. If you are ever forced to defend yourself against these extreme circumstances, you may use the BLACK EXPERIENCE as a blueprint.

HELP!

If We Do Not Cherish This Beautiful Black Skin, Who Will?

Our peers gravitate toward our culture like loyal supporters. So many nationalities relate to us because, according to science, they originate from us. The first creation skin tone was tan and beautiful not beastly or barbaric. The globe is dictated by the flamboyance, fashion, and influence of blacks in popular culture. We are permanent ink that stains the world's perception of life, liberty, and love. The black experience has been lapped by the field, and we still present the most unique talent to our civilization. Economies around the world would go bankrupt if we chose to balance our needs, wants, and necessities. If we chose to consolidate currency and control compassion, our future endeavors would be able to address our children's empty college funds. If all Americans feasted off of love, minorities would not be looked upon as second-class citizens. We live in a society that exploited the energy of a people for profit. The almighty dollar controls the opportunities for beautiful black babies. Yet a rebellion will not secure a single dollar for our descendants. If we rebuke and rebuild race relationships, we may have an honest chance to co-exist in a country that has never accomplished that task.

CHAPTER 6: WHEREWITHAL
(BY ANY MEANS NECESSARY)

Why Are We Persecuted for Being Black? The Dominant Color of the Rainbow Is Looked Upon as a Blemish

Malcolm X made me proud to use the terms black, African, or Afro-American. I am in a state of bliss when I look in the mirror and see the bronze of beauty. The skin tone represents several shades and mixtures of brown with streaks of color from one end of the spectrum to the next. The black experience covers the entire rainbow from the light of dusk to the dark just before dawn. World history commands we gave birth to ethnicity, culture, and civilization. We educated the entire Earth about the energy of devotion. We traveled from Africa to every corner of the globe. We are the color God began the rainbow with, so there is no logical reason to be ashamed of being black.

HELP!

We Do Not Realize the Power in the Words We Write, Speak and Comprehend

We must re-educate the world on the value of our own story. We must share vital information that we own—the only true version of our past, present, and future. We can no longer stand by and allow distorted pictures to be painted of our people. The abstract vision of enslaved black men, women, and children has the whole world entertaining that we were savages. Check with your scholars, scientists, the Internet; your research will explain it best. Who was the first civilized human being to walk this Earth? Do not guess about history; know your history because if you do not educate yourself, they will tell you anything.

CHAPTER 6: WHEREWITHAL
(BY ANY MEANS NECESSARY)

Divide and Conquer? Have We Been Separated from Our Land, Liberty and Bloodline?

Has the separation of souls fueled black-on-black crime in America? A nationality without a past presents a confused citizen by nature. We were brought to this land by force under inhumane conditions. The affluent African heritage issued wherewithal to the Negro (formally known as African) who was made to crawl through the terrain of torture and live as beasts. We remain in this American wilderness as Afro-Americans (formerly known as Negros) surrounded by wild beast; if we tread carefully, we can avoid the hunter's attention. The rich soil of Africa has grown the economy of many wealthy empires around the globe. Settlers stole soil by landing on Africa as if it were the moon, planting their nation's flag and shoveling the wealth from this extraordinary continent into their pockets. It is time for the black experience to extract evil from our earnest energy, from the coast of Africa to the mountains of America.

HELP!

Will the Black Experience Accept Amnesty from America?

What dollar amount would balance the slave trade? Would the descendents even acknowledge an apology? Forty acres and a mule misled the ex-slave into Jim Crow's "equality." Reparations are needed in a country that has ravished its own economy. The black experience must invest in land when the interest rate allows ownership. Land is the wealth of all nations. A great number of revolutions and wars have been based on territory (land). A conversation regarding reparations reminds a descendent of guilt that their forefathers carried. The world is due a bill for taxes, penalties, and interest for the black experience in America.

CHAPTER 6: WHEREWITHAL
(BY ANY MEANS NECESSARY)

The Side Effects of Slavery Has Shackled Our Souls Far too Long; Injustice Has Crippled Our Imagination

We can no longer afford to stand timid on the sideline and complain about the corruption in society's competitive race. When you choose not to participate, you also choose not to have a voice in the outcome. We have become complacent in our quality of life, willing to bend with the wind. The man who is fed up and goes against the grain will be the same man labeled an outcast, traitor, or enemy. It only takes one brave man to stand for justice, but it will take the entire Supreme Court to solidify justice. It seems so simple to stand firm in justice and not allow the highest bidder to auction off human rights. We must capture peace, unity, and equality in order to operate a world with justice for all people.

HELP!

African Heritage Began to Break Down on the Love Boat, Dissolved Further on the Plantation and Now Has Completely Vanished in the Afro-American Community

What makes some African and Caucasian Americans so ashamed of being associated with Africa? More importantly, what makes some people so ashamed of being a part of the black experience. I've witnessed several individuals claim to be a mix with Indian, Caucasian, Asian, Latino, etc. It seems some reach for another nationality not to be a 100 percent descendent of Africans. There is no one pure race because God created different cultures to witness that we live as one nation. The original tribe God created exhibited the tone and pigment of color. A barrier between races is the creation of man. Racism, hatred, and jealousy are manmade, not God created. The destruction of the human family tree is also the work of man. If you do not resemble your neighbor, it does not mean that he is not your relative. How can any of us hate the root from which we came?

CHAPTER 6: WHEREWITHAL
(BY ANY MEANS NECESSARY)

Justice Allows the Soul to Remain Silent, But Injustice Ignites the Soul and Vents Vandalism

The soul is humble by nature, but society has created misery in the souls of many individuals. Trust has become a distant memory among people. Respect seems to linger on life support, while hate is healthier than ever. Dignity has dissolved into dishonesty that avoids the consequences of its acts. Honest people are far and few in a nation of frustrated families. Some police patrol areas they did not grow up in, do not live in, and despise having to work in. Cops should have a connection to the community they police. If protect and serve were really practiced, police brutality would vanish. Once the black experience refuses to accept anything but respect, all nonblacks would be forced to take inventory on how they interact with the black experience. We have accepted financial, mental, and physical abuse for far too long. We may have to remove our revenue from the pockets of the Pilgrims.

HELP!

Wake Up; the Hands on the Grandfather Clock Move Quicker Than You Realize

Father Time will leave you holding decades of your life in your hand if you are not careful. We can no longer hope and wish for adequate change. We have to architect action into accomplishment. We have to seek a union headed by honest human beings who share humility with the less fortunate. The cause the people support is balanced with consequence and correction of risky behavior. The task won't be simple—to challenge an establishment—but the conditions suggest do or die. Waiting and allowing time to motivate has resulted in limited success; sacrifice will push the envelope. We would be wise to invest in education because an entrepreneurial mind is unlimited. The recipe for the successful future for our children consists of past family excellence and present-day determination. Our black experience will be only as strong as each individual's desire to achieve.

CHAPTER 6: WHEREWITHAL
(BY ANY MEANS NECESSARY)

Help Us! Who Will Come to the Financial Aid of the Black Experience?

The black experience with the assistance of our good friend, the Caucasian, finds our urban community behind the eight ball. When there is no true chief, the Indians run wild and only focus on individual teepees. The Indians once blamed the pale face for communities that are leaderless, careless, and confused. The black experience stumbled out the gate with the weight of America on our back, but perseverance balanced our people. The race of life is a marathon and all the sprinters are out of air, but with a brisk pace and endurance, we will be victorious.

HELP!

I See It in Your Eyes;
You Are Afraid and Frantic

Fear flows freely through your veins like the Nile. When I ponder the word fearless, the first image initiated in my mind is the immense Malcolm X. Can you imagine being blessed to converse so eloquently from the soul? Can you even appreciate being able to experience his several lifetimes in one life? He donated his own life for his religion, race, and relatives. A man's wealth begins with the addition of his word, and he does not allow any dollar amount to subtract his honesty. The value of Malcolm X to the black experience was a solid investment and created inflation in the pride, dignity, and respect of a passive people. Malcolm X's passion opened the color blind eyes of a nation. He personally knew the pain of being a black man; he'd lived the life and survived the mean streets. A man of the struggle is an expert witness that karma chose not to prosecute. I have adoration because Malcolm X promoted power, passion, and purpose in the spirit of the black experience. May minister, forefather, and honorable El Hajj Malik Shabazz educate the next evolution of leaders!

CHAPTER 6: WHEREWITHAL
(BY ANY MEANS NECESSARY)

Aspire — Now!

We have no control over the will of the next individual's soul; so why do we continue to attempt to control their behavior? Utilize the exhausted energy previously spent on someone else to replenish your spirit. Life is not corrupted by coincidence, and it is impossible to escape faith, which is a follower of our decisions. Do not stand by as the last grain of sand slides through the hourglass without any ambition in your life.

HELP!

Is There Anything Left to Fight For?

The black experience in the sixties assumed it had TKO'd Caucasian supremacy with an assault of body blows. It believed it had hit racism at its core. It unified the black community and instilled an energy to counter any attack. But we are now one-half century removed, and our momentum has evaporated just like our illusion of instant freedom a century before. The hardship and stress people encountered for the civil rights of all American citizens seemed null and void, until a black man was elected president of the United States of America in 2008. The right to vote had been disrespected by those who refused to vote until a historic election energized a nation. Do not stop now; we must continue to vote to elect qualified individuals who will not let politics pressure them into abandoning their promises. If we get lackadaisical again and lower our guard, we may not have another chance to vote, march, or demand justice. Whether you admit it or not, the struggle continues.

CHAPTER 6: WHEREWITHAL (BY ANY MEANS NECESSARY)

The Only Tool the Black Experience Needs to Construct a Solid Foundation Is Family. Now Is the Time to Architect an Alternate Plan of Action

The black experience has birth multiple powerful nations, from kings in Africa to slaves in America. Where would America be in the hierarchy of world superpowers without the free labor of the black experience? If America the beautiful blessed society with an honest answer regarding the importance of her illegitimate child, racism would commit suicide. The blueprint is simple: work as hard for yourself as our ancestors worked for a nation that continues to neglect their grandchildren's necessities. We have the intellect to control our education! We have the skills to manufacture our own goods and operate our own industries. We live in a society that only respects producers, and as long as we continue to buy and not produce, we can wave bye-bye to our dignity. If we begin to trade goods, we will be able to balance out the wealth in our great country. The black experience has made its mark in history for centuries, and now the demand is to secure space on the throne in the near future.

HELP!

Our Actions Do Not Seem to Move in Union with Our Promises; Our Accountability Is a Long Time Coming

We have compromised culture, land, and our self-preservation, right here in the land of the free and the home of the brave. For far too long, we have avoided the side effects of mental, physical, and financial abuse from an economy to which we gave a luxury tax credit. After investing our entire existence into the wealth of America, we are no longer good enough to be looked upon as second-class citizens. We have allowed immigrants to accept the Constitution after we fought for equality and move their businesses into our communities. We pay their wage to push us around. We do not control the services or the products in our own backyard. We have made a limited impact as role models, but we can make a significant stance as parents. Our children's future depends on the decisions we make now. Our black experience must embrace unity, or our race as we know it will face extinction.

CHAPTER 6: WHEREWITHAL
(BY ANY MEANS NECESSARY)

The Black Experience Is in the Best Position Possible: 'The Underdog'

What better time to sneak attack your target, than when they are filled with arrogance and at ease? At the end of the eighteenth century, Toussaint L'Ouverture led a rebellion that empowered the first black nation in the Western Hemisphere (Santo Domingo, Haiti). Nat Turner led a rebellion in 1831 that cost him his life for the opportunity to enact freedom for his followers' families. History has a habit of repeating itself when karma equilibrium is out of balance. Would you rather rise and fight for the conditions of all people or will you continue to turn the other cheek as a semi-free man? The options are up to debate with physical, mental, or spiritual warfare depending on each person's agenda. At any cost we must protect ourselves and our interests. We must organize. The Good Book explained it best: " The last should be first and the first should be last."

HELP!

We Must Recycle Revenue into Our Own Communities

The net worth of our investment in the free market is zero. Confidence in color seems to be negated due to the black cloud that follows the black business owner. Skeptics say security is limited when lending currency to potential black business risk. Black consumers should consult their conscience when they shop. What businesses are you supporting? Not supporting black business confines our culture. There is no mutual respect between black revenue and nonblack enterprises because they know we will spend anyway. They can continue to remove black currency from our communities because we castrate black business with greed and jealousy. From franchises to mom-and-pop establishments, all the way up to corporations, they will be forced to respect our opinion, once we decide to remove our dividends from their wallets. We can rebuild our communities and create urban landscapes where black professionals stand side by side. Our revenue has to pass through our black fist, more than just once. We can not assist any business that will not lend a hand nor a dollar to create continued currency for our children. We must demand the respect that our black dollars are capable of commanding.

CHAPTER SEVEN

Self-Defense!

Chapter 7 is a self-help chapter. It is designed to continue the complex charisma of chapter 1 (Love Thyself). You will be challenged, and you will face challenges as you secure your environment. This seventh entry focuses on your reaction to circumstances that do not instantly go your way. Can you remain humble against actions you cannot control and people's opinions of your actions? Will you believe in your faith when questioned by experts who complicate your perspective? It will give you the tools needed to resolve conflict and control conversations you find yourself in. The secret is the control of self; once you remain constant, you can control all people, places, or things in which you come in contact. Your foundation will command respect, and that is a greater quality than being liked or even loved. Once you have matured and realized everything is about YOU, you have educated yourself on SELF-DEFENSE and now are qualified to utilize your black belt against the habits that still hinder your destiny.

HELP!

Even the Wise Man Who Gallops Along a Smooth Path Encounters a Bump in the Road

However, the secret of the wise man is how quickly he mounts the saddle and continues his journey. Expectations are the thieves of self-esteem. The road of life is filled with potholes and rough terrain. There is no way to escape unexpected pitfalls, but with faith in God you can withstand adversity. God stands on His own, but we cannot stand upright without His balancing hand. If you wish to be true to yourself, put faith first, and your reward will amaze you.

CHAPTER 7: SELF-DEFENSE

The Will of a Man Is Only as Strong as the Spirit of a Man; Temptation Feasts Off Weakness and Lack of Willpower

Do you think it is possible for the mind, body, and soul to be effective without a union? Does self-control or even self-discipline play a role in your life? How many promises to yourself have you walked away from? Do you have a grain of willpower stored in your spirit? It is okay to answer any of these questions with a yes or a no, but is it not okay to then not correct the error of your ways. When you are not honest with yourself, the first person you hurt, cheat, and destroy confidence in is you. Your faith is crucial to your confidence, courage, and strength. Your connection to God has to be valid, vivid, and vigilant to endure the pressure of temptation.

HELP!

Even with Hindsight, You Cannot Envision the Emergence of Emergencies, So with What Value Do You View Your Life?

Are you prepared for an emergency? You can not plot or graph on a chart unforeseen conditions dealing with life. Even the great country of America does not provide health coverage for all its citizens. Do you keep your health in mind when you interact with people you encounter? Germs, bacteria, and disease are transmitted through needles, fluids, and bad sexual behavior. It is your life, so it is your job to maintain a clean bill of health. The extracurricular activities you participate in today will affect your health conditions tomorrow. Alcohol, cigarettes, and drugs create an altered being for the moment, but when you abuse them, that altered being becomes a lifetime scenario. God has not issued a gauge to anyone to monitor the span of their life. That's why you should appreciate each day that you wake in good health and enjoy each evening that you rest in good health.

CHAPTER 7: SELF-DEFENSE

A Cliff Can Claim a Leap of Faith or a Sudden Slip into Demise

As I listen to the ground break beneath my feet, I silence the sound to secure my stance. It is not a coincidence that a choice comes at a timid time, but I am lifted by belief. I am superhuman, and I am awaiting an abundance of certitude to collect esteem. Reality begins to reign as the rain of doubt decides to attack past behavioral defects. It is impossible to waiver an individual once he realizes the realm of his destination. Your wildest dreams are only an eye-opening experience away, so wake up and the thoughts are yours to explore. If you bother belief just for second, you will believe destiny has an offer you can not refuse.

HELP!

There Are No Escape Routes When Reality Runs the Helm

Sometimes it takes a minute to realize the condition you've allowed yourself to be in. The control of the mind begins with the behavior of the human being. The direction, or the lack there of, dictates the feelings and emotions of the confused soul. A plan participates in the healing process of the lost individual. Joy only eludes people who depend on others to grant them happiness. Sometimes the best quality time is spent alone to ponder on your next move in life. It would be wise to establish a genuine relationship with yourself, so you will be able to offer a mate a person of substance. If you do not enjoy your own company, who will? The mask of contentment that many of us parade to the world only disdains a true peace of mind. Faith will always be a foundation that can bring heartache and pain to a halt. Set your mind to achieve success, and your heart will allow you to accomplish it all.

CHAPTER 7: SELF-DEFENSE

Being Distant Can Ruin Your Reputation in Relationships

Relationships are tricky. People cannot know what you are thinking if you don't tell them. Appearing distant can harm any relationship; it can sow the seed of gossip and rumor. All too often people take rumor as fact; they pass judgment without getting both sides or investigating concocted claims. Gossiping is easy; finding the truth is hard, sometimes the hardest thing you will ever do.

HELP!

What Is the True Price of Success? Achieving Our Goals Does Not Come Cheap

We all have to pay in one way or another before we anchor any achievement. To obtain any form of success, you have to display discipline, dedication, and diligence. Currency is not always the cost of success. Life is like a cashier that accepts hard work, sacrifice, and determination as payment. Life will not accept excuses, lack of willpower, or quitters as legal tender; you must pay your debt to society on time. We are all obligated by God to offer a helping hand, once we achieve any form of wealth.

CHAPTER 7: SELF-DEFENSE

There Is No Obstacle That Bears the Same Strength as Our Will

The odds will remain in your favor as long as you keep your goal in mind. Procrastination drives us down a one-way avenue to a life filled with barriers. Emotions pamper perceptions that lead to the easy way out. Can diligence deliver urgency that allows goals to lie at the doorstep of success? The correct choice can command a course of action that will lead to your wildest dreams becoming reality. Focus on a fixed goal that will enable you to jumpstart your self-esteem. The nature of man is to succeed and strive for excellence while basking in faith.

HELP!

Honest Effort Develops into Success and Excellence

Failure should serve as motivation to pursue your goals even more. If you put forth your all and fall short, your work ethic will ease your conscience. Procrastination is a risky borrower of time; we can not afford or extend accommodation in our effort to keep pace in a slumping economy. Life has no limits when you aim to overachieve. Determination will guide you through the darkness and allows willpower to be your light. You have to invest time in your dreams and goals to receive a payoff. Why do we expect so much out of life when we are not willing to sacrifice to accomplish even the small tasks in life? Allow your imagination to ponder on unlimited possibilities and then go after these thoughts with tenacious effort. Life's rewards will be granted when the guidance of God is appreciated.

CHAPTER 7: SELF-DEFENSE

Do Not Allow Anyone's Opinion to Wage War on Your Self-Esteem

When you maintain an honest perception of yourself, no one can rattle you with their thoughts. Some individuals enjoy, embrace, and endorse misery as a part of life. Unhappy people create love-hate relationships with anybody who crosses their path. The power frequency is both positive and negative so a balance is needed to maintain emotions. Arrogance and cocky behavior do not represent self-esteem, pride, and respect. The most confident man is the man who stands humble because he has nothing to prove to the world. Some of us spend a great deal of energy speaking harshly against others in order to dodge our own low self-esteem issues. When you focus on your own life, you do not have the vigor to surveil someone else. An opinion should never intercept the potency of your goals, especially when the idea is not your own. The only opinion you should accept with open arms is God's because faith will never lead you wrong.

HELP!

Is Your Image Your Downfall?

It does not matter what people think of you, but the opinion of others can disrupt relationships. Points of views, perspectives, and perceptions can cloud the character of the individual. The way people look upon you may not be the same way that you see yourself. What vision are you projecting to the world in which you live? We have to keep in mind that when we follow the leader, we always fall behind. Once in a while, it's wise to reflect on the individual who stares back from the mirror. Reality checks should be random and realistic. If you have not become who you wish to be, consider a change to become what you want. One's personality can persuade people's opinions of who they think you are. Embrace the person who you are or change the demeanor you display. Through faith, love for self builds self-esteem. Love for self can finally create an image that people cherish. If we are willing to be honest with ourselves, sometimes we are what people perceive.

CHAPTER 7: SELF-DEFENSE

The Past Is a Constant Reminder of Both Good and Bad Memories; Life Will Allow You to Grow If You So Choose

Do not harp too long on your mistakes because time is on your side. You have a choice to correct your errors in life and change your ways. Do not be fooled; no one is perfect. When you find a person professing to be perfect, point them out, so the world can witness their actions. In the meanwhile, pick yourself up, dust yourself off, and head in a positive direction. The change starts with you!

HELP!

The Past Is a Hurdle We Must Clear to Enjoy the Track of Life

Use your past as a compass to maintain a forward direction. Do not allow past failure to dictate future endeavors. Build your foundation on solid ground filled with reality. Evict all self-doubt, self-criticism, and self-denials. Stimulate your mind with a positive thought pattern—I can, I will, and I want to grow from my mistakes. Do not continue to relive every failure. You must figure out a way to forgive yourself and let it go.

CHAPTER 7: SELF-DEFENSE

I Will Never Quit, Forsake or Renounce Success

Success usually doesn't come too easily without faith. If you are not prepared to go the distance, the race of life will wear you down. There will come a time when you lavish, linger, and love what you have accomplished. This will be the moment when you must maintain the enthusiasm toward your goal. I believe too many of us celebrate before we have actually tasted success. We allow ourselves to enjoy the present and disregard our future. Some seem to abandon goals at the fork in the road. This is also the point where we tend to travel in the direction in which we've come. Some seldom realize the progress they have obtained until they have made a U-turn. The struggle begins on the climb up the mountain, and to maintain momentum, you must display discipline. Once you reach the peak and choose not to continue an arduous work ethic, an avalanche will smother your self-esteem. Rejoice and celebrate the fruit of your hard labor, but do not lose focus while you pass out party favors.

HELP!

As the World Spins, Time Tends to Separate Souls from One Another

The people we love sometimes change into people we do not even know. The people we once admired as children can now be considered equals as adults. The rest of the people we know live out their lives; so new people we have yet to encounter can begin theirs. We as people should be willing to accept the change in others as long as we mature with them. Sometimes people can change direction, which can dictate the outcome of tenured relationships. You have the right to grow, even when it affects the people who surround you. If you can not find people in your existing circle to embrace the change you choose to make, then solicit new friends to support you.

CHAPTER 7: SELF-DEFENSE

Finesse Finds Friends, While Arrogance Walks Alone

Pride can isolate you. Your inner strength may be perceived as being overbearing and not capable of being polite. It is critical to govern confidence because first impressions can sway your chances in building new relationships.

HELP!

How Do You Face Adversity?

The way we embrace problems will mold our attitude toward the world. How do we handle frustration? What choices do we make in times of controversy? These are the things that establish our lives. Destiny delivers faith to help us. The agitator who avoids arrogance may still be able to adapt quietly to change. Life will lean toward the lessons to which we apply the most weight. Behavior challenges the conscience to a duel, while failure attempts an attack on our beliefs. A chainsaw reaction will accelerate the words that define our demeanor. Perception ignites the friction that burns the bridges of friendships. When we assume, we remove common sense and logic from our opinion. The true test comes when our tempers flair and we are forced to deal with the unexpected adversity. Always remember this: the actions of others can not dictate our reaction — unless we allow them to.

CHAPTER 7: SELF-DEFENSE

Trial and Error Is the Cause and Effect That Silently Summons Excuses in Life

Focus, courage, and endurance energize the essence of our accomplishments. Perseverance is the only armor required in the war of distraction. Allow your imagination to attack any chore your dreams left not covered. Visualize your new attitude filled with value, vigor, and variety. Imagine your new self and new spirit being blessed by the grace of forgiveness. There are rewards for making drastic changes even though initially you can not see them clearly. The prize is a new beginning, a step in the right direction, and, most importantly, less baggage for your new journey. Life will only be what the individual makes of faith and choices.

HELP!

A Thief Can Torment Your Talent But Will Never Be Intelligent Enough to Steal Your Ideas

There is no human being, manmade machine, or creative thought sufficient to embezzle what an act of faith has created. Why wonder what could have been? Allow your aspirations to dominate. If you do not take notice, people will envy your accomplishments until jealousy demolishes your relationship. It is wise to interview the individuals you are considering taking into your alliance.

CHAPTER 7: SELF-DEFENSE

We Have the Energy in Our Soul to Turn Any Wrong into a Right

Oppressors can only control that place and time of oppression, while the healing of the wounds can begin internally with a state of mind. We do not choose to be victimized, but the choice is ours to remain a victim. If you spend your life concerned about the corrections others suggest, then you will auction off your self-esteem to the most obnoxious opinion. You and only you have control over your mind, body, and soul. Do not allow your kindness to cause you to live as a victim of circumstance.

HELP!

Peace of Mind Allows an Exit from the Wicked Ways of the World

Do you enjoy the sweet sound of silence? Your home should offer peace and harmony to your soul. There is no one but God who can enter your space unless you allow them access. We can no longer allow another individual's anger to filter into our energy. You must expand the healing of happiness because grace has been garnished in our complex society. Your spirit will shine with bliss and set an example for all unhappy people. A smile is a gentle gesture of compassion from one person to the one in need. Anger is nothing but frustration that people refuse to deal with on a humble playing field. Faith offers a path of peace, but all too often man chooses a road of rage.

CHAPTER 7: SELF-DEFENSE

Are You a Pawn on the Chessboard of Life?

Who is in control in your life? When you are in charge of your life, your actions will be the source of your power. Do not give your power to a powerless person. We all crave the chance to be a constituent of a crusade that celebrates when checkmate is gestured. If you can only move in a space that has been designated by disguise, then your fate has already been predetermined. If you plan and know what rules are relevant, you can capture any kingdom that attacks you. Know your position; do not allow the game of life to control your next move.

HELP!

Charisma Can not Energize a Course of Action Alone

Religion, relationships, and reality spark passion in our daily lives. Normally, the excitement of a new year will motivate people to seek change—like lose weight, find a different occupation, enhance their education, or get in tune with their higher power. The choice to command change is priceless, but the course of action has a small fee attached called sacrifice. When faced with sacrifice, many people will allow the flame to burn out so they can return to their original state. Your will has to force procrastination into submission. Theologians through history maintain man was created in the image of God, and there has been no greater winner known to man than the Almighty. If that's the case, then why are so many of us not content with our present status in life? You dictate your happiness and success until you relinquish your faith to the next God-fearing man. We have all been blessed with the emotion within us to choose our own path and the ability to follow that choice through to the end.

CHAPTER 7: SELF-DEFENSE

Perception Pollutes the Mind with Madness, Mayhem and Mischief

Our mind will allow our vision to see what it wants to see. Our behavior is dictated by our view of circumstances. Often we tend to react before we even understand the act of another. The terror, turmoil, and torture we endure due to mistaken belief are avoidable if we control our interpretations. Our feelings take the blunt of the abuse when we perceive an event to be negative when in actuality it's not. The thought of an individual who does not walk in your shoes should never shame your spirit. The only perception we should be interested in is the one of the Creator. I suggest we walk through life and only deal with the facts. Root out all fiction to better understand one another.

HELP!

You Can Only Not Be Yourself for So Long; Your True Nature, Thoughts and Actions Will Always Prevail

Why do we venture into relationships and play an award-winning role? We sell a dream with our best behavior, just to reel them in. Once we have them on the hook, the standard we set initially is a difficult pace to maintain. You should allow yourself time to establish a friendship with complete honesty. If you want a relationship to succeed, make sure you are willing to be flexible and open. Most importantly, develop yourself as a person before you make your next commitment.

CHAPTER 7: SELF-DEFENSE

My Mother Explained to Me That Love Is an Action Word and That the Love You Seek Is the Love You Are

I believe true love is the discipline to love thy enemy. You have the option to hold a grudge all the way to your dying breath. You can be a bigot, hating everyone not like you. How logical is it to dislike or even despise someone you've never even met? The best option for all of us is to learn how to forgive and let it go.

HELP!

When You Choose to Peel Back the Layers of Pain, Sometimes the Depth Will Disappoint You

An individual with an attitude has allowed pain to control his compassion. We have all experienced an event in our past that has left a hole in our soul, which time has yet to heal. Your whole life can revolve around that event, or you can accept what you can not change and move forward. Once we accept adversity and allow our minds to manage memories, the past does not doom the present. The future will find a way to prevail, and the pain of dealing with the past will be a figment of our imagination.

CHAPTER 7: SELF-DEFENSE

Our Mental Capacity Dwarfs Our Physical Capabilities

A man can move a house with his mind, but he can not climb on top of the same house without a ladder. The mind can process the steps required to reach the top of a mountain, with or without legs. The brain can bet against fate and lose a limb, but the body can not afford to wager and lose its mind. The cerebellum can not allow the immune system to take a second off. The mind must plot the coordinates of toxins in the body so the cells can attack and rebuild the body back to health. If the mind allows the body to deteriorate from poor health decisions, is it murder in the first degree? Life is a joint adventure, and the connection of the mind, body, and soul can not be taken for granted anymore.

CHAPTER EIGHT

Bad Habits Die Slowly

Chapter 8 compels our characteristic for accountability. Why with all of this vital information are we now questioning our own behavior? If we do not address human nature, then we are not being honest with ourselves and, unfortunately, must return to the beginning of chapter 2 (Where Do We Go From Here?). It takes time to become insecure so why would it not take time to master being secure? This eighth entry is a result of an individual's request to rectify his actions by excuses. Once you establish a routine and choose to part from your natural necessities, you will revert back to what's comfortable from time to time. Do not beat yourself up; just make sure you have checks and balances on your own behavioral patterns. You will eventually remove most of your detrimental behavior but do not under estimate the energy of evolution. Do not get too at ease because the same behavioral defects that you have control of, a lot of individuals do not and their BAD HABITS can have a negative impact on us all.

HELP!

When Will We Stop? The Second We No Longer Have an Option

I have been waiting a long time to move forward, but I have hesitated every step of the way. Change seems to battle my passive behavior, and I continue to surrender to the pressure. I wish, hope, and wonder for a new beginning, but emotions refuse to tackle the timidity that holds me captive. The next day becomes yesterday because I have not prepared for tomorrow. I no longer think about the joy of life; I only act like I am enjoying the life I have. I have had enough, and now I am ready to remake my world into something wonderful. It can start today, so I will make a choice, support my decision, and stand by my side to the very end.

CHAPTER 8: BAD HABITS DIE SLOW

One Compulsive Choice Can Induce a Spiral of Sorrow

God loves us through the lessons of our lives. God has many ways to alert us of the danger that lies ahead. God tames our short attention span with tact. Even when we are stubborn to obey faith, God will isolate the good and bad behavior for us. A split-second decision can detour your life and lead to self-destruction. A selection made with haste in mind might mingle with mischief. We tend to allow trouble to tantalize our imagination while turning our world upside down. Faith causes a derailment on the track of temptation. A man's preference sometimes places him in harm's way and often adds self-imposed humiliation. The castle you create should not contain a drawbridge that collapses on you, when you enter and exit. Caution can control the choices that create turmoil. Once we begin to plan, our thoughts will process our actions and lead to a precise conclusion.

HELP!

Trouble Lurks When You Lose Focus and Live for the Moment; We Can Not Afford to Take a Break from Discipline

Procrastination is detrimental to progress. Once you take a stride in a forward direction, do not go backwards in life. Bad habits linger in submission, while positive change struggles to become a regular routine. Hard work and dedication are mandatory, if you wish to obtain the best results in life. Longevity is the pace to maintain self-discipline in this life of temptation. You have to shovel deep within you to load the hazardous behavior that needs to be dumped and demolished. Success is the vision of victory of a goal. A man's word is the only property he truly owns. Material trinkets lose worth, while Father Time whistles "Dixie." Time can not be recycled. I suggest you utilize each second because time only matters when you run out of it.

CHAPTER 8: BAD HABITS DIE SLOW

Temptation Breaks Down the Spirit of a Man; Blasphemy Breaks Down Our Faith and Connection with God

Your path is unclear, unguided, and unfulfilled when you tap dance with temptation. Your vision is blurred by the sight of frustration, heartache, and pain, when you stray from what you know in your heart to be righteous. While God has all the control, man has choice. We will enjoy prosperity through passion, purpose, and prayer. Give one day to God, and in return, you receive a lifetime. Will you be steadfast in our Savior or will you relinquish your power of choice?

HELP!

Who Is the Enemy within Us?

The cliché says the angel and the devil will both hold claim to a shoulder as long as we fiddle with our faith. God's mercy and grace never give up on our lost souls. God will empower you with strength to endure any weakness, enticement, or addiction. Still, we crave the excitement of this life over salvation. Your conscience will guide you. Listen to it. You are the creation of a choice that commands answers. Karma knows exactly what direction to point us in when we are lost in the translation of truth. It is a behavioral defect to choose things that we know are no good and that's the enemy in us. Do not blame anyone else when you realize what's right and you select what's wrong anyway.

CHAPTER 8: BAD HABITS DIE SLOW

An Untamed Thought Is Like a Wild Stallion Running Rampant Through Your Mind

Are you conscious or just careless with ideas that contain contradiction? Indecision does not allow your mind to flourish. If you are adamant about avoiding anguish, do not allow your thoughts to get caught up in controversy. Keep your ideas innocent. Once you allow a conspiracy theory to groom your thoughts, your mind gallops away. Step off the road to reckless action; choose careful thought over impulse. There are millions of thoughts to decipher every day, just process the ones filled with bliss and demolish those that are detrimental.

HELP!

The Food We Eat Dictates Our Mood and Emotions

If it were up to us, most of us would live for an eternity. So why do we persist in eating poison? Why do we pump pollution in our bodies with alcohol, drugs, and poor health habits? Our body cannot function properly when it is fueled by poison. Overeating, binge eating, and obesity all lead to low self-esteem or, even worse, depression. Starving your body is no better than filling it to the extreme. Seek balance in your daily diet. Many Americans claim that they love themselves, but by the way we eat and destroy our bodies, you would never know it. Your mind, body, and soul all need an adequate appetite to coexist as one.

CHAPTER 8: BAD HABITS DIE SLOW

Discipline Does Not Deny You Quality of Life; Impulse Does

Addiction disarms us. It lulls our internal army to sleep until we have no one to protect us from self-inflicted self-hatred. The indulgences you may find comfort in may be the same items that continue to hold your happiness hostage. We find it easy to berate our neighbor's poor habits while we disguise our own. Soberness will deliver your destiny the second you make it a habit.

HELP!

Seeing Past Illusion to Belief

Your state of being and acceptance of your soul begins with your own chosen belief system. The glare of a second opinion may obscure your view. Even the tumultuous thoroughbred cannot stay focused on brilliance without the help of blinders. The foolish follow too closely causing a blur to the backside of a jackass. Speaking of hindsight, a blind spot may hinder the illustration of innocence. A helpful hint may aid those who remove contacts but are still blinded by a cock-eyed matrix.

CHAPTER 8: BAD HABITS DIE SLOW

Excuses Are Exceptional Circumstances, But Success Shares Neither Compassion Nor Concern

An insincere effort receives only an ovation of ire. When honesty is absent from the arena, those who applaud are left feeling empty. It is only an act when the performance is based on pacifying perception and brandishing bravado. When the fictional farce begins to play on the intelligence of the crowd, they will demand a drawn curtain. A true impersonator will always camouflage his performance—even to the point of mimicking the main character—to avoid accountability.

HELP!

While Lip Service Tries to Fool Someone Else, It Is Really the Act of Fooling Oneself

Leadership is of no importance when you mislead yourself. Our ego sometimes allows arrogance to dictate our expression through gossip. We exert all our energy talking about action, and then we spend no effort honoring the act. Honesty commands a clear conscience and offers balance to candid conversation or a passionate point of view. A person's word is the value of his or her integrity. If you can not be taken at your word, then you have little chance of gaining someone's respect. People do not respect a person who only bluffs a good conversation but never accomplishes a single task. Make sure your words have value, and you back them up with true action.

CHAPTER 8: BAD HABITS DIE SLOW

Do Not Believe Everything You Hear; Beware of Gossip and Slander

There are few people who are willing to offer a positive frame of reference. If you are driven to know something about another person, then ask the individual who is involved. You should never imply, insinuate, or insist upon facts that are foreign to your personal business. There are too many experts on other people's business and affairs. Analyze your own concerns, and if you are honest, you will find something about yourself that needs correction. Remember, the Good Book says, "Thou without sin can cast the first stone."

HELP!

Gossip Gathers Dust as People Begin to Choke on Their Words

Some find humor in reciting speculation that has been circulated through the ears and lips of many. It seems so simple for insecure individuals to spread fact or fiction about family, friends, and foes. The rumors would wash away if we chastised careless comments when we heard them, if we quieted the questions with answers of facts. We indulge in conversation that we would want no one to mention if we were the culprit. We use the social environment to entertain our ego and boost our self-esteem. We would not want others to speak of us in such a distasteful manner, so why do we participate in spreading the pain of others? Why do we receive extraordinary enjoyment from the breaking news of our neighbor's turmoil? We should respect the privacy of each and every individual we come in contact with. We should hope that our peers would regard our private information with the same security that they regard their own. One way to eliminate gossip is to not participate in it and to penalize those who do. If we truly are interested in disposing of gossip, we only have to send in silence.

CHAPTER 8: BAD HABITS DIE SLOW

Remove Emotion and Judgment and Open Your Mind!

Your opinion may devastate someone's outlook because you failed to gather all the facts. Sometimes people do not want your opinion. The personal experience that they have shared with you is not always open for debate. Sometimes people just need to share their secrets—without scrutiny. Do not pass judgment on others; karma will be kind enough.

HELP!

Learn from Life's Lessons or Continue to Retrogress in Reality

The student exclaimed experience is the best teacher. I begged to differ and asked: what if you did not acknowledge the experience? We are lost when we dawdle in detrimental desires that have caused harm, hurt, or humiliation in the past. We treat life as a gamble and embrace the jackpot of pain. Security begins when we no longer allow the past to affect the future. We should embrace the past, not continue to reminisce and drown in sorrow. The days of giving energy to complaining are done. There is nothing positive that can come from second guessing. We can learn to appreciate a lesson or continue to wallow in its liability and consequences. You must allow yourself room for error, or you will beat your self-esteem into submission. We must walk away from our lessons with a sense of gratitude and grace for our Creator's unconditional love.

CHAPTER 8: BAD HABITS DIE SLOW

Time Is Up! Have You Once Again Waited to the Last Moment to Manage Your Time?

Time is so sensitive that being late takes the next second for granted. If you continue to put off now for later, your success rate will hit bargain basement value. Deadlines are Russian roulette to the individual who continues to shoot procrastination into his veins. So give thought to preparation and say good-bye to pressure. If you stay one step ahead, you will always have room to stumble and remain on pace. The effort we put into a task will ultimately relinquish the reward we are seeking. Anything you choose to do in life will follow you, so present yourself as a person who is of high character and dependability. Promptness separates the pupil from the pack and will guarantee that you will make the grade.

HELP!

I Have Traveled too Far to Realize That I Am Going in a Circle

If you are not adamant about bringing change to your life, you will continue to stall and spin your wheels. I now know change is a work in progress, and sometimes it is frustrating when you do not maintain momentum. When you allow your mind to recollect about the past, your body opens a door in the present and your soul shuttles bad behavior back to the future. The cycle begins and ends with you. Honor your commitment. A promise is no more than a sentence if you do not follow up with action. A goal or a plan can assist in the success you seek and plot a course out of the cycle of an unfulfilled life.

CHAPTER 8: BAD HABITS DIE SLOW

Moving Backwards Only Alarms You When You Realize You Are in Full Stride

The wrong choice disrupts your life and activates your growing pains. Lessons are to be learned from; they remind us of boundaries we have set to awaken us if we are faced with this choice again in the future. Are you willing to compromise your present accomplishment to learn the same lesson again? If lost in foolishness, utilize direction that you already know has guided you in dealing with this foolish behavior in your past.

HELP!

A Helping Hand Handles Generosity with Calm, Compassion and Class

What will you do when karma returns to remind you of all you have not done for others? One day you will have to acknowledge achievements that were accomplished with the help of your supporters. Once you have established success, you have to remain humble and share the gifts a fortunate life provides.

CHAPTER 8: BAD HABITS DIE SLOW

The View May Vanish When You Focus on Someone Else's Horizon

We seem to waste energy on what was not done instead of appreciating what was. Someone can do nine out of ten things correctly, but we will hone in on the one unfinished task every time. We never use the same judge and jury on our own faults as we use on people we hold in contempt of court. We will either adapt to appreciate someone's effort, or we will one day be a victim of our own criticism.

HELP!

Today Begins, Even Though It Seems Like Yesterday Will Never End

The clock has struck midnight, the Earth has continued to circle, and your obstacles have organized to offend accomplishment once again. We refuse to believe in time travel, but we all have traveled between space and time. An individual who looks back on what could have been and does not exile those demons will forever be one second behind. If people would accept their present condition and be willing to share their secrets to success with the naïve naysayers, maybe we would be able to break the cycle, move forward, and start a new day together.

CHAPTER 8: BAD HABITS DIE SLOW

A New Year Does Not Guarantee a Different Outcome, Only Another Chance

I am going to change this year, but I will not do anything differently than last year. I will wish, want, and wait on happiness but refuse to love myself. I will wish for the best the world has to offer, but refuse to embrace reality. I will want all the trinkets my greed can create but refuse to appreciate any of it. I will wait on my blessings but refuse to pray and become obedient. Life can be filled with contradictions, if you allow your mind, body, and soul to abort another New Year's resolution.

CHAPTER NINE

Hell on Earth (September 11, 2001)

Chapter 9 suggests that society take a look at the separation caused by its riches, racism, and rush to judgment. A national disaster can cause a nation to reconcile its past behavior for forefathers who have left hatred for children to sort out. This ninth entry is dedicated to all individuals who have lost their lives to senseless violence of politics and foreign policies. The people have limited choice but to suffer the burden of the outcome. People are faced will difficult decisions, but we must choose right for all people or our people will continue to suffer HELL ON EARTH individually. You have to look to a DIVINE power to sort out the salivation our minds cannot comprehend.

HELP!

Today Is the Day I Choose to Give Life, Not by Seed But by Salvation

Today marks the first anniversary of September 11, 2001 (Hell on Earth) and my twenty-eighth year of existence. My date of birth is now infamous and synonymous with a country's pain. It is our duty as a nation to embrace 9/11 as a national holiday, to remember our loss of beautiful innocence. The victims' families will forever fantasize about this day, imagining what it would have been like if it had never begun. My humble recommendation is faith based and saves souls that were sacrificed for ignorance. Some years have passed since 9/11, and some people are not as passionate as they once were. Still, we can not allow our citizens to carry the burden of foreign policies again. Our choice has to rejoice in justice, or we will be victims of a variety of evil people.

CHAPTER 9: HELL ON EARTH
(SEPTEMBER 11, 2001)

A Few Courageous Citizens Are Required to Wake Up the World; People of All Nationalities Must Unite

Future leaders of America, are you willing to lend an ear to the concerns of our Third World brothers? A good word to a refugee in need of sovereignty is only a breath away. The diction of dominance projects entitlement and assassinates confidence; it creates hatred in the hearts of men. The war continues to multiply murder and only brings sorrow to families. There is an all-out attack on the last superpower known to civilized man. Nine-eleven was the tip of the iceberg that isolated innocent Americans from life. When anger is built up and forms energy, it has the capability to destroy nations. Unfortunately, our foreign policies have made more enemies than allies and brought the wrath of war to our soil.

HELP!

Does America Represent Democracy to the World? The Wealthy Would Agree While the Poor Would Beg to Differ

To many, the past and present policies of the United States of America do not sound the pleasant tone of equality. We are a nation that enslaved people. We are a nation that oppressed people on our own soil. Freedom is financed by birth and not by an allowance from an amendment attempting to correct an iniquity. Economics has allowed men to absorb power and tamper with the true meaning of salvation. Greed has allowed men to separate human beings by race, religion, and region. World supremacy has allowed nations to black out entire populations in an attempt to purify their land. To no avail, the world is getting darker and the sunny days are numbered.

CHAPTER 9: HELL ON EARTH
(SEPTEMBER 11, 2001)

When Will We Wage War on Domestic Terrorists: Irrational Cops, Racists and Rapists?

Since 9/11, America has not hesitated to flex political and financial muscle on international terrorists. So why, since the formation of the thirteen colonies, has America stood so silently by as Americans terrorized other Americans for centuries? Neither the Justice Department, the Supreme Court, nor any other government agency created "by the people and for the people" has secured the civil rights for all people. How many more taxes do Americans have to pay to finance the salaries of senators who seldom support their constituents? How many more breaking news stories does America have to endure before she admits a problem on her own soil? What continues to drive racism in a country that was structured by diversity?

HELP!

Racism Is the Evil in the Garden

Society will never grow as a whole as long as our individual souls are planted in a dry soil. Why are we stranded in the desert of life? Because we do not want for others what we demand for ourselves. Our Almighty offers an oasis only when we participate in peace, love, and serenity. Your religion of choice does not grant you an exemption from right and wrong deeds. Some believe a "righteous" cause is a blank check to create chaos at any cost. The seeds of hatred have bloomed in fertile soil in all corners of the world. The weeds of destruction have begun to blossom out of control and suffocate the surrounding roses of peace and goodness. Nine-eleven brought in a bad crop of spoiled values and rotten morals, and the consumption of these fruits has made all of us sick to our stomach. Our behavior has brought the hot spots of the world to a boiling point. Which nation will be foolish enough to spark World War III?

CHAPTER 9: HELL ON EARTH
(SEPTEMBER 11, 2001)

Corruption Denies Access to a Clear Conscious. At What Cost Does the Individual Sell Out Integrity for Advancement?

What have we done to prevent parasites from invading our soil, which in return will hinder our harvest? America always seems active in foreign affairs and eager to provide financial aid to fellow allies. Who was there to help the innocent Americans, when the Twin Towers came crashing down? We are one of the most sophisticated nations in the world, and we did not anticipate our own planes piercing through the sky to bring devastation to our own people. Who was there to assist the helpless residents of New Orleans when Hurricane Katrina knocked at the Gulf Coast's door? We now must direct our focus and funnel our tax dollars to American families suffering so horribly during this economic crisis. Do not let the smoke settle before you realize our foreign interests do not share the same importance as our domestic interests.

HELP!

Trickery Taints the Law of the Land and Jeopardizes Justice for All

History repeats itself as America manipulates the truth. Our country seems to evade ethics while chastising the world for not being ethical. Superpower status has made Americans lenient when it comes to our own immoralities. Society has mastered the art of judgment through unjust jurisdiction. Decade after decade, we continue to demolish decency in our democracy. Our world views are voided by our victims' vendettas against our foreign policies. The wicked ways of a few has the whole world weary of the red, white, and blue. Our Constitution carries little value to the aid of the minority class or poor white people. The good old USA must tie up loose ends with the black experience before it attempts to help the rest of the world. America must honor the words of our founding fathers and place our John Hancock as written proof.

CHAPTER 9: HELL ON EARTH
(SEPTEMBER 11, 2001)

Are We Blinded or Do We Tie Our Own Blindfold?

The building has collapsed with us in it. What was the thunderous noise above us? When will we realize that everything is not quite what it seems to be? Nine-eleven was a nightmare that took the lives of angelic people. Man has manipulated and caused mayhem on the Earth to the point that some men believe the only solution is senseless violence. Man has displayed an unbelievable hatred for the existence of his brother. The Earth has become flooded by the tsunami of greed, and the globe no longer holds enough sea to drain the overflow. Man and our relationship with sin have created hell on Earth for it patrons. What motivates a man to become mute to murder? What is inside a man's spirit that creates the act of a savage? What has man done to remove the humbleness in his heart that heals all troubled souls?

HELP!

What Does It Mean to Be Intelligent, If You Continue to Isolate Yourself from the Truth?

The individual who fell victim to the same attack twice obviously did not anticipate being taken advantage of again. An education offers an opportunity to excel in life and a chance to defend your principles against the educated. Common sense is free and does not come with high regard, but it offers an outlet to compromise with scurrilous people. It's one thing to read and retain what you read, but it means a magnitude more when you read, comprehend, and then execute your own intelligence. If you continue to allow the world to manipulate your brilliance, then you symbolize a person of ignorance and do not recognize what is unfolding in your presence.

CHAPTER 9: HELL ON EARTH
(SEPTEMBER 11, 2001)

Everybody Seems to Want What Everybody Else Seems to Have

On the outside gazing in, the view is vibrant and nothing looks out of place. But the individual who resides in this glass house suffers from the same sickness as the person with his nose pressed against the window. The individual who looks out views the beautiful landscape, which lays outside the slightly cracked window, and thinks it must be paradise. The illusion that the next person's life is better than your own can damage the perception of your own life. There is no perfect person, and all people experience episodes of negative energy. If we would only address the circumstances that pertain to our passion, then our neighbor's outcome would not be important in our mind. You have to nurture your nature with love, and it will blossom right in your own yard.

HELP!

A Quiet Calm Can Combat Voices That Plot Against Your Vision of Victory

People will plot, but your belief can never display hesitation. Your path will have to be carved through the discipline of your courage. Your desire has to develop twice the passion as the individual who despises your diligence. Your desire for happiness is your goal, and this gift will never be wrapped with a bow and presented to you. Here is your choice: take control of your peace of mind or allow people to pick your reality apart.

CHAPTER TEN

Divine Guidance!

Chapter 10 positions your faith to finalize your belief in a higher power of yourself. This tenth entry is intended to magnify the blessing of chapter 3 (God Help Us). When in need, you call on faith because you did not maintain a connection when things were going good in your eye. Normally, you fight your lessons every step of the way but claim to be a believer of Divine Guidance. It is the result people seek and not the patience it takes to manufacture miracles. It is the mentality of faith that issues heartache, not the emotion because emotion will allow you to believe when it's good or bad. Once you exercise belief on its highest frequency, your connection with God is yours to enjoy, and you are not afraid to share it with the universe. Finally, a force field of energy will enter your existence. The results are Divine Guidance because you believe in YOU.

HELP!

The Attributes of Faith Alarmed My Soul by Forsaking My Fear

The soul complies with the will of faith, when the conscience waivers, wonders, and whittles. Faith arrays humanity with mercy that negates the forces of nature. The power of God should not be mistaken as passive because that perception will leave you powerless. Lost souls linger in despair, while faith adjusts our attitude. A faithless individual's life stands still, barren of accomplishments while the flesh wrinkles away. Revelations of faith riddle our beings with blessings that benefit us. The fear that should be exhibited toward God must be filled with faith. Fear lies parallel with love and limits the longevity of faith. The only fear that should ever be displayed is that toward God.

CHAPTER 10: DIVINE GUIDANCE

The Only Favor God Asks of Us Is Cleanliness of the Mind, Body and Soul

Positive energy is the shield that defends the mind from a negative way of thinking. Our imagination battles our belief when we feed it negative ideas. Our past is only detrimental to our self-esteem when we ponder on past failures. Recovery begins when we clear our mind and cleanse our thoughts of mental torture. Actions are what the body craves from the operator. Fitness is the foundation to good health and the enjoyment of your physical life. Your body is the engine that uses natural energy to navigate through the road of life. Faith secures the safety of the soul and solidifies salivation. Faith demands that fears exit and make way for the spirit to soar. Faith allows the individual to repent and the soul to be saved. Faith balances the soul and creates harmony with nature. The mind and body will eventually fade away, but the soul of the individual lives forever.

HELP!

Are You Ready for the Unthinkable? God Issues Lessons in Bundles

We are seldom ready for the consequences of our choices. There are always warning signs, but we do not always embrace them. God beams balance to a turbulence-filled life. Our conduct constantly displays that we do not believe until God allows karma to force our own will upon us. People will enter and exit your life, but sometimes it takes solitude to appreciate your blessings. Life will heckle you as it drags you through the desert; then it will reward your sacrifice, stress, and strain with a mountain peak of success. Life can be biased even when you are honest, humble, and helpful to fellow human beings. Embrace life's lessons and life will always be worth living.

CHAPTER 10: DIVINE GUIDANCE

Only Credence Can Save Our Lost Souls from a Tailspin

When in trouble, we fall to our knees to appeal to the throne for salivation. Life is a lesson that delivers the information that God allows us to intercept. Our common sense is cursed by temptations that our flesh embraces. We tamper with thoughts and ideas that are detrimental to the existence of our freedom. We sometimes believe we have escaped the law of nature and the law of man, but the grace of God has given us another chance. Karma can chastise the conscious when we allow our emotions to act subconsciously. Enticements can create envy that allows an individual to lose poise. In an attempt to maintain temperament, we must exercise our faith and follow our chosen connection. Man has only confused the text that has been sent for his own redemption. The world will continue to debate as long as we lack the will to utilize logic. Plant your faith in God—never in man—and watch your beautiful life bloom with bliss.

HELP!

Devoutness Is the Way!

It does not matter what language flows from your tongue. It does not matter what name you call God. It does not matter what religion you cherish. We all have the God-given right to choose different paths to search, seek, and save our souls. Our salvation will only be granted if we meet the standards of divine guidance. We call God a list of different names; some in Arabic, some in Hebrew, and some in Greek. In your most electrifying dream, you can not imagine the diversity of our Creator. Keep in mind, if you truly cherish the denomination of your choice, you must ponder that the day will come when you will be judged on the principles of the religion that you claim to worship.

CHAPTER 10: DIVINE GUIDANCE

Now May Be the Last Opportunity; You Have an Option to Convert

Just because you rise does not mean you are awake. The jury does not pass judgment on your past indictments; the verdict will be rendered by your lack of innocence. Kismet keeps account of all our deeds, be they pure or evil in intent. There is a place of glory once your lungs have taken their last breath. You are obligated to live by laws, even if the law does not serve and protect you. You are bound by books of testaments brought by believers of a higher power of justice. Man and woman are to respect the quality of being in a union that requires paying dues. The law of the land has been corrupted by criminals while holding the Holy Bible hostage. Plea bargains vanish when we expect mercy and yet are not sincere in our request for leniency. Do not allow your time to pass because history does not reduce a life sentence of guilt.

HELP!

Man Has a Limited Role in His Own Make-Believe Manuscript of a Life

God allows man to whisper in the form of prayer to hear his cry. We navigate our opinion by the choices we make, which alerts God of our voice. A little leeway is allowed but will never allow you to go too far off course. Mercy and grace seem to secure our lost souls from our own greed. Love will float as a life preserver amid the wreckage in emotional storms. We gain glory in the eyes of purity by fondling faith with our spirit. Only the Supreme Being can brush the masterpiece of life so gently that it rights all wrongs. The insight to innovation is viewed first by the Creator who then gives inspiration to the individual. Each soul is a minute piece to the puzzle that God is working here on Earth.

CHAPTER 10: DIVINE GUIDANCE

I Am a Man of Miracles Motivated by the Spirit of God; I Live My Days to Satisfy Salvation

I am a philosopher, poet, and patriarch. I am an advisor, analyzer, and architect of words. I am human, humble, and a healer of lost people. My passion runs rapid through my soul with every new word that blooms into a thought as beautiful as a red rose. My life is now committed to communication to bring about serenity of the mind, body, and soul. When I express myself, I am blessed with bliss, nobled by peace, and one with the Ruler of the universe. I said all that about me to argue this fact about you: you can accomplish anything you wish, once you make up your mind and then put forth an honest effort. Life is worth living once you choose to live.

HELP!

I Was Blessed to Begin Another Morning, So I Must Live This Day by Faith Not by Fear

Fear destroys the desire to live in peace. Fear is the feeling that floods the veins with low self-esteem. Fear is only an embrace by God in the form of admiration toward him. Faith is the destiny you encounter when your blessings begin to flourish. Faith is the confidence to achieve any goal your imagination can conjure. Faith is the total submission to righteousness and the will of God. Faith can stand toe to toe with any addiction and trip temptation by denying weakness of spirit. Faith moves forward, while fear fades away!

CHAPTER 10: DIVINE GUIDANCE

The Love You Are Is the Love You Seek!

My mother explained to me that I came from the love she dreamed of. My mother conceived me at a very young age and, like so many young girls, yearned for love. Do you believe it was a coincidence that my mother, my sister, and even the woman who gave birth to my daughter, all had children at a young age? The father's position in the family is to demonstrate the desire to love unconditionally. A father who plants a seed and does not help educate the roses he helped create can pollute the soil that will eventually harvest the world. A lost young girl, a bitter single parent, and a strong educated woman, all have the opportunity to birth the next great man. My mother has accomplished all three.

HELP!

Words Can Not Begin to Describe the Joy, Passion and Happiness I Feel in My Soul When I Think of My Mother

I celebrate Mother's Day every moment my lungs process breath. There is not a day that goes by that I do not thank God for the eloquent woman that He blessed to be my mother. Mother, with the guidance of God, you've directed me when I was lost in the wilderness. Mother, with the guidance of God, you have instilled courage, dignity, and intelligence in my life. Mother, with the guidance of God, you have showed me that a person can achieve anything he puts his mind to. Mother, I love you with every grain of my spirit in my soul. Enjoy this day but keep in mind that every day is Mother's Day in my life.

CHAPTER 10: DIVINE GUIDANCE

My Mother Explained That God Allows Old Flames to Venture Back into Your Life So You Can Realize You Have Not Missed Anything

God has created a detour to embrace closure by letting go. The past is a distant memory of events that can stunt your growth as an individual. There is no manual lever on the hands of time. You can not change what has already taken place in life. It does not matter how long you ponder on your concerns, the circumstances will not change. The decisions that you have already made are your history, and the choices you make today are your present. Your future will hold whatever success you sacrifice to achieve. You can not enjoy the blessings of today, if you continue to live the sins of yesterday.

HELP!

Happy Birthday, Son, You Have Been the Sun to Me for the Last 365 Days

The light of my life has the same facial features that I have. Why do our nose, feet, and hands display so many similarities? Our emotions rage the same way when we feel ignored, isolated, or inadequate. I covet your passion when you do not get your way because I am demanding myself. How could two be so much alike but eventually will be so different? We share the same zodiac sign being born between August 31 and September 11. I will offer you principles that will sometimes frustrate you but, ultimately, will free your mind from worries. You have pierced part of my heart that now floods my soul with joy. I will always be there for you Cyncere Gregory Arnold, because God's mercy blesses my darkest days with a son.

CHAPTER 10: DIVINE GUIDANCE

You Represent the Angel God Sent to Spare My Life; You Are a Gift from the Heavens

My Savior sent me a blessing, small in size but humongous in heart to wake me from a detrimental sleep. This beautiful individual was disguised as a soul mate to suggest that I participate in a soul search. I sincerely apologize for the prison of love I chained you in as I struggled through my many fears. The woman I dreamed of was lost to the insecure individual that I once was. I am a new man in many ways, but I still have to balance the old habits daily. When I choose to involve my behavior with bad habits, you always seem to be there. That's the reason I know God loves me and that He sent you to be my angel. I pray one day that I am blessed to be an angel to someone in need, like you were for me. You must continue on without me to spread your wings and love for the next lost soul in need. I will always love, remember, and appreciate my angel of love.

HELP!

If You Are Able to Walk the Balance Beam of Life, You're One Step Closer to Your Blessings

I only seem to waiver when I fumble with my faith. My words and actions do not always move in sequence. My intentions are noble, but sometimes I live selfishly. I pray to possess a spirit of passion and purpose to deal with my ancestors' pain. I live too much for today and not enough for tomorrow. I spin emotionally and get dizzy, but God always brings me to a stop. I have a love for lost people that drives the hurt in me to change the world. I do not like what society is doing to our children, so I must take a stand and prepare for the worst. I will sacrifice my well-being for the seed that will grow to infect this troubled territory. My nation is numb to the black experience that has been hindered by racism, classism, and colonialism. Our job is to help rebuild the structure of the black experience, so we will be able to lead the world by example.

CHAPTER 10: DIVINE GUIDANCE

Frustration Favors Failure Because Frequently Freedom Fails to Fondle the Mind

Life does not choose the lessons we encounter, but in hindsight, we blame life for our choices. Turning a blind eye to the truth becomes a habit to those who wallow in denials. We often allow our fears to defeat our confidence and condemn our future. Many of us distort our destiny only to demand drama, disorder, and heartache. We refuse to take our submarine souls to a depth deep enough to float toward freedom. Freedom is what you as an individual equate to being sincere to self. Once we remove the chain from the library, knowledge will then escape to freedom. The mind develops at a rapid pace with free information. Education frees the mind so utilize your head.

HELP!

The Love of a Woman Is Eloquent and Everlasting; God Chose Woman to Be the Mother of the Earth

A woman's passion for her husband, her children, and her social environment are impossible to measure. She nurtures by nature. Women are the vital to the growth of our children. Women play a major role in the qualities instilled in good men. Our history explains it best, women are known for grabbing the bull by the horns and fighting for justice, equality, and peace on earth. Words can not describe the role of a woman.

CHAPTER 10: DIVINE GUIDANCE

What Religious Doctrine Holds the True Account of Divine Prophecy?

Has man been manipulated by a fancy fairy tale to worship false deities in order to be controlled by faith? Has man purposely distorted the word of God for his own benefit? Has man tampered with the books of God to give glory only to himself? Has man's imagination and ego allowed him to believe the work of God is his own? Has man's attempt to clone animals given him the false pretense that he is God-like? Man is made up of the mind, body, and soul in the image of God, but he is not God himself. Man will one day approach his Maker and indeed make amends for his sins. We must pay respect to the Creator and all His gracious creations.

The Truth about Lying

There are three types of people in the world: those who tell the truth, those who lie, and those who tell the truth or lie according to which benefits them. A person who is honest can be trusted to a degree, but no one is perfect so look to their actions to dictate your relationship. A person who chooses to lie can not be trusted by their word, so watch their actions — their actions will always tell their truth. A person who is indecisive tends to waiver; you cannot trust either their actions or their words.

CHAPTER 10: DIVINE GUIDANCE

Passion Protects the Path of the Passive!

We only know our own truth. The reality of a lost wish is only fantasy unless you choose to believe. I know where I stand today, but I do not know how to accomplish what I need to live tomorrow. The distance between the dream and the reality that will deliver access to the door of success is blocked with doubt. Make a plan to take your time and cut the master key because a short cut of picking the lock will always leave you locked out. Your beliefs, if you plan accordingly, will carry you when you are insecure and do not know which direction or course of action to take.

HELP!

The Great Gift of Giving Grounds the Soul

Our heart was created to pump compassion for the less fortunate. The man who gives has just as much pain as the man who receives. A man with a conscience can not live with comfort, as long as he knows he has not made a contribution to society. We all have the duty to fend for our families, but we also have a responsibility to respond to our community's needs. The selfish soul is duped by greed. God mandates miracles through the spirit to spread love and serenity. The heart of the individual initiates the grace to grind kindness with kinship. We must wake up from greed, or our souls will continue to slumber.

CHAPTER ELEVEN

Bliss!

Chapter 11 commands the celebration of supreme happiness. You can now see your hard work has led you to ABUNDANCE. You are not concerned with things that bothered you before. You have serenity, you have peace of mind, and your life has a certain calmness. You have limited the negative energy that once surrounded you. Now your positive energy infects people who admire you. You are a difference maker, you have helped society, and you are blinded by BLISS! This final entry is a collection of my motivational memoirs that I have shared with our global community.

HELP!

Bliss Beckons — Will You Answer?

I can have whatever my dreams desire. Happiness floods the shore and leaps to the top of the cabanas. Money has become a hurdle that can no longer slow my pace because I'm jumping over barrels of cash. Wait a minute; I have managed to discard the weight that I no longer cared to carry. I am a self-published multimillionaire who writes motivational memoirs. I am a life concierge, keynote speaker, and well-respected hero in my community. I am the best father I can imagine being, and I am a dedicated husband. I am a successful son who has helped his parents. I am a friend; I am a brother; I am a wise man. I have accomplished all the greatness in my mind—and so can you! Live through my journey and create your own because I am willing to share the secret.

ABOUT THE AUTHOR

Gregory V. Arnold was born on September 11, 1974, the son of a single teenage mother living east of the Gateway Arch and Mississippi River in East St. Louis, Illinois. He was well traveled in the first thirteen months of his young life, moving back and forth across the river between East St. Louis and St. Louis with his grandmother, mother, and her siblings. Eventually, Gregory's young mother and father followed tradition and utilized the Arch as the gateway to the west to Los Angeles, California.

Gregory matured quickly in the sophisticated streets of South Central Los Angeles. After his young parents decided to part ways in the big city, he drifted between parents absorbing his mother's compassion and charisma and his father's wit, humor, and work ethic.

Gregory took to the streets as an honest hustler and enjoyed the energy of entrepreneurship. He ventured in performing arts as a young performer of poetry and rap music. However, the more Gregory peddled for profit, the more his GPA and credits plummeted in junior high school and continued to fall the freshman year of senior high school. Worried about the agony-filled path his child was on, Gregory's father stepped in with a healthy dose of discipline, direction, and LOVE. Gregory went on to complete two years of senior high school in one year and graduated high school on time.

HELP!

Since then, Gregory's appreciation of education has prompted him to attend community college where he was introduced to his passion of public speaking. Gregory's artistry was also rekindled through writing as he penned his first manuscript (HELP!).

Gregory perfected his people skills during the last seventeen years as a leader in corporate America. In addition, Gregory has spent the last seven years as an operations manager, where he has become an expert on the behavior and motivation of people.

Today, Gregory stretches his entrepreneurial wings with the creation of his own brand, HELP! (Help Me, Help You, Help Us). He is an educator and a visionary with an extraordinary story that connects the past, present, and future. A servant leader, Gregory prefers to think of himself as "a life concierge, not a life coach." He is engaged to be married with three children and a beautiful supporting family.

HELP ME, HELP YOU, HELP US!

Thought-Provoking Questions

HELP! is about self-introspection and self-motivation. Consider these questions as you work on the project that is you. Write down your answers and reread them as you make your way through this book.

Do these circumstances apply to me?

Am I a part of the problem or am I part of the solution?

What can I do to expedite a positive outcome?

PRAISE FOR HELP!

Greg,

I thoroughly enjoyed your book sample, and I would like to express my appreciation for the opportunity to read it. The topics covered in the book were so engaging that I lost all track of time. It was well-written and contained sound, practical advice. In fact, I have already benefited from your discussion on "fitness being vital to the longevity of life." I believe the topics will help your readers realize that our problems are typical, and we can solve them in constructive ways. I think the book will be a great motivator to many.

By any measure, you are a very effective writer and educator. I found your comments regarding constructive criticism, African heritage, and "God help us" especially intriguing. Your material was written in a way that everyone can understand and will induce universal interest.

Thank you for sharing a memorable "presentation of literature." I look forward to reading your next informative work.

Arnetta E.

P.S. In addition to speaking to students, have you considered communicating your work on the radio?

PRAISE FOR HELP!

Hey Greg!

Hope all is well with you! I'm still reading your material, and I'm truly impressed. I'm really learning that I need a major "overhaul" and to make Kita happy first! I will give you my thoughts and feedback when I'm done. Thank you for sharing the draft of *Help!* with me!

Dynomite reading so far. Heading to chapter 2 this week.

Bobby H.

Everyone at any level in life should read this book! *Help!* can put you on the right track or aid you in lending a hand to lift others! Greg's positive energy is beyond refreshing and I feel so fortunate to be exposed to his wisdom, compassion and inspiration! *Help!* truly motivates the Mind, Body & Soul!

—R.J. Baldwin-Ford

AWARDS AND HONORS

Dear Gregory,

Congratulations! The epic results are in for the National "Best Books 2009" Awards! Your book has been honored as a "Finalist" in the "Self-Help: Motivational" category!

HELP! (Help Me, Help You, Help Us!)
by Gregory Arnold

Finalist

Self-Help: Motivational

Your title will be listed live on USABookNews.com for an additional six months.

From the Mel Robbins Show

Congrats (for being a finalist)

Cambridge Who's Who Registry of Executives, Professionals and Entrepreneurs honored Gregory V. Arnold and Help Enterprises in its 2009–2010 edition.

ABOUT HELP ENTERPRISES

HELP ENTERPRISES MISSION: "Help is not a handout based in emotion but a course of action connecting our commitment to our communities through compensation."

HELP ME (BUSINESS): Help Enterprises is bound by our Help Me, Help You, Help Us philosophy. Our company is committed to the care and awareness of the less fortunate by franchising financial freedom. We will utilize the 360 degrees of recycling revenue to compensate our world community. It is not our goal to accept handouts, but it is our agenda to aspire assistance. We hope to motivate others, reduce the financial aid needed by our society of citizens barely surviving on a fixed income, energize entrepreneurship, and boost self-esteem in the process.

HELP YOU (BLUEPRINT 360 DEGREES OF HELP RECYCLING): We will buy, sell, and trade as a world community, which will attack the core of poverty.

HELP US (BENEFIT): Compensation is the key that opens the federal reserve of unlimited resources. It is not always a cash value that validates an individual's validity. Charity and nonprofit organizations are crucial because they facilitate communication and chemistry between the fortunate and less fortunate. Help Enterprises will remove all barriers and bureaucracy by soliciting the significance of helping individuals in need of basic necessities.